Bello:
hidden talent reaiscovered

Bello is a digital only imprint of Pan Macmillan,
established to breathe new life into previously published,
classic books.

At Bello we believe in the timeless power of the imagination,
of good story, narrative and entertainment and we want to use
digital technology to ensure that many more readers
can enjoy these books into the future.

We publish in ebook and Print on Demand formats
to bring these wonderful books to new audiences.

www.panmacmillan.co.uk/bello

Edith Olivier

Edith Olivier (1872–1948) was born in the Rectory at Wilton, Wiltshire, in the late 1870s. Her father was Rector there and later Canon of Salisbury. She came from an old Huguenot family which had been living in England for several generations, and was one of a family of ten children. She was educated at home until she won a scholarship to St Hugh's College, Oxford. Her first novel, *The Love Child*, was published in 1927 and there followed four works of fiction: *As Far as Jane's Grandmother's* (1928), *The Triumphant Footman* (1930), *Dwarf's Blood* (1930) and *The Seraphim Room* (1932). Her works of non-fiction were *The Eccentric Life of Alexander Cruden* (1934), *Mary Magdalen* (1934), *Country Moods and Tenses* (1941), *Four Victorian Ladies of Wiltshire* (1945), *Night Thoughts of a Country Landlady* (1945), her autobiography, *Without Knowing Mr. Walkley* (1938) and, posthumously published, *Wiltshire* (1951).

Edith Olivier

NIGHT THOUGHTS OF A COUNTRY LANDLADY

First published in 1943 by B T Batsford

This edition published 2014 by Bello
an imprint of Pan Macmillan, a division of Macmillan Publishers Limited
Pan Macmillan, 20 New Wharf Road, London N1 9RR
Basingstoke and Oxford
Associated companies throughout the world

www.panmacmillan.co.uk/bello

ISBN 978-1-4472-6626-6 EPUB
ISBN 978-1-4472-7200-7 HB
ISBN 978-1-4472-6625-9 PB

Visit www.panmacmillan.com to read more about all our books
and to buy them. You will also find features, author interviews and
news of any author events, and you can sign up for e-newsletters
so that you're always first to hear about our new releases.

TO THE
STRANGERS
WITHIN MY GATES

PREFACE

Like most living creatures, Miss Emma Nightingale possessed two distinct personalities. In her case, they were the Emma-by-day, and the Emma-by-night. The night creature was certainly less savage than are some of what are snobbishly termed the "lower animals". Nobody would confuse her with the lion roaring after his prey; with the cat wauling unreservedly for a mate; or with the owl filing the air with doleful hootings while he floats round the barn after mice. No. Miss Nightingale went early to bed; and, once there, she lay quietly, unaware that she was, in some curious way, quite another person from the familiar figure known to her neighbours as they met daily in the village street.

Most people suffer a "dream change" of some sort, though they generally enter it before they are actually in the world of dreams. At nightfall, the most civilised and conventional people revert to the animal, nestling into bed to revel in the sheer physical pleasures of soft pillows, clean sheets, and hot-water bottles. Love and lust are both more potent at night, as the Hebrew poet knew when he wrote, "I sleep but my heart waketh". And the spirit too wakes into a new quickness, as the body grows drowsy. Many people, in the small hours of the morning, scribble passionate lyrics of supreme beauty; only to find, next morning, that daylight has washed the beauty away, leaving only ashes. The poignant tragedy of our little lives overwhelms us during wakeful hours of the night. We become King Lear, or the Duchess of Malfi; and by morning we realise there is nothing dramatic about our small worries. They boil down to a chronic inability to balance the debit and the credit sides of our personal accounts.

Then again, how brilliantly amusing one is at night; and we often laugh loudly at our own jokes, so long as there is no one near to make us tell what we are laughing at. No doubt, both sense and spirit are more alert at night, this is how it came to be that Miss Nightingale's war-time reminiscences naturally take shape as "night thoughts".

She was one of those cultivated and "county" old ladies to be met with in most villages—supremely interested in local affairs, generous to the poor, stern to the evil doer, pardoning to the penitent. She was a leading spirit in all local activities—Church Council, Conservative Association, Women's Institute, Girls' Friendly, and Brownies. She also "lived her own life", as they say, for she did not consider herself to be altogether of the village. She had moved in wider circles. Her father had been a well-known writer in his day, and his friends had been distinguished people. George Du Maurier was Emma's godfather, and, on her drawing-room wall, there still hung a pen and ink sketch of her as a little girl signed by the famous Punch artist. During the summer Mss Nightingale still entertained at week-ends, in the little house put at her disposal by the Squire, those of the friends of her youth who were alive. She was not well off, but she had never thought of taking in "Paying Guests", and only a European War could have driven her to such a revolution.

Cut adrift from her old regular ways, and ardently seeking means for putting into practice the high-hearted patriotism in which she had been nurtured, Miss Nightingale now filled the house with strangers, and in the night she mused on their strange ways. She was accustomed to writing at night, for her parents had taught her to write a careful journal. When she went to bed, she always put down in as few words as possible the actual events of the past day. She made no comments. Who would read this, she never thought. The existence of her diary was well known to her friends, for it often came in useful when there was a disagreement in committee, as to which evening in the previous February, the Girls' Friendly had begun their Lenten working-parties. Except for such utilitarian purposes, the growing pile of books was never disturbed. Miss

Emma did not find her old journals interesting; and she had taken the precaution of tying a large label round the bundle which reposed on the floor of her wardrobe. It ran thus:

TO BE DESTROYED UNREAD WHEN I AM DEAD

Yet when the war drove her to fill her house with strange guests, it also drove her to fill her diary with strange thoughts. For the first time in her life, she did not merely enter the names of her guests. She wrote down who they were, why they had come to her house, what they were doing, and how they behaved themselves; for these seemed to be the most extraordinary things about them. In the past such details would have been superfluous, for she knew all about her visitors. Everything was taken for granted. No stranger came to stay. And now the remarkable thing about her guests, and indeed about her whole life, was that it, and they, were strange. In this, Miss Nightingale's experience was shared by village people all over the country. This broadened hospitality, and these unaccustomed contacts, completely changed for the time the character of English country life.

During a recent "Salvage Week" in our district, Miss Nightingale arrived one afternoon in my house, bent down beneath the burden of between fifty and sixty large cloth-bound exercise books. They were tied together, with, still attached, the forbidding Notice as to their undisturbed destruction.

She handed me the parcel.

"Here is some very good salvage," she said.

I knew what the books contained.

"Can you part with them?" I asked. "Aren't they valuable for reference?"

"Not now, I think. Everything is changing so much that we never need to refer to the past. It doesn't apply."

I was seized by a sudden tenderness for this bundle of notebooks. I knew how much it contained of Mss Nightingale's life.

"I believe that in the future, we shall often have to look back

to see what we did in the past," I said, "and your diary has generally been our only book of reference."

"It doesn't apply now," she repeated in a sad voice. "The last three years are the only ones that count, and even with those, the Council Clerk gets so many new instructions (over six hundred in six months, he says) that the notes in my diary about what we did two months ago, are now completely out of date. It has no value except as salvage."

I saw by her face that it had cost Miss Nightingale a great deal to sacrifice her diary, and I felt that a little respite might make it easier for her.

"The last three years," I said musingly. "We might find it very useful to be able to refer to those. I suppose you wouldn't allow me to look through them before they are finally destroyed?"

I could see that this suggestion was a relief to Miss Nightingale. She was fond of me, and had confidence in my judgment.

"Read what you like, and make what use you like, of what you read. I am not dead yet," she continued grimly, "so that Notice hasn't come into effect. But you will see that I am right. My old diaries are not going to be of use to anybody now."

She retained a purely utilitarian attitude towards her diaries, and I guessed that, as far as that was concerned, she was probably right in her estimate.

I watched Miss Nightingale go down the garden path and through the little gate, and she seemed to be changed. She had lost something from her brisk youthful walk. She had left a part of herself in my house with her diaries.

I sprang to my feet to say one last word. The last three or four volumes of the diary had been on my lap, and my sudden movement sent them settling to the ground. Even the noise of their falling did not attract her attention. She would not look back. I watched her go.

I never saw her again. The next morning, the whole village was shocked by the news that Miss Nightingale had died suddenly in the night. Perhaps I was less surprised than anyone. I had been troubled all the evening by that last glimpse of her when she left her diaries behind in my house. It seemed that she had consciously made an end.

I decided to interpret her last words to me, as making me, in some measure, her literary executor. I carefully read all the volumes through, remembering that she had trusted me to deal with them as I thought best; and now I felt that she had said the true word about her diary.

"It doesn't apply. The last three years are the only ones that count."

She was entirely right, in so far as she had looked on her diary as nothing but a summarised Minute Book of all the organisations to which she belonged. It had had its use. We had often proved this; but now it was extremely dull and she had been wise in thinking that it had better be destroyed.

But with the beginning of the war this diary of hers had completely changed its character. In it, she had described her journey from Derbyshire on one of the last days of August 1939, as "a Watershed". It was to cut the landscape of her life in two, and now I saw that it had also cut in two the character of her diaries. If I were to call the later volumes "post-impressionist", I might arouse false expectations. Miss Nightingale's writing in itself could never have that character. But I use the word as it is defined in the Oxford Dictionary. It is there said to apply to work "in which the representation of form is subordinated to the subjective view of the artist". This is the change which came over Miss Nightingale's diaries during the last three years. Her subjective views appear for the first time.

I believe that in their new form the diaries do "apply". They give a picture of one aspect of rural life which during the war came into being in many country places—I mean the effect upon them of the influx of strangers in their midst. So disturbing a change did not fit into the stiff and formal mode of Miss Nightingale's previous diaries. Yet she was impelled to note it down. But instead of the curt notes recording merely each day's engagements, she now described in some detail what had actually happened. She wrote what she thought about what she did. This writing is like Miss

Nightingale's private talk with her friends. Sometimes she was rather a racy conversationalist, and now her records of the coming of the lodgers, and the way in which the village entertained them, reproduced some of the spice of her personality.

I have compiled this book from what she actually wrote in her final volumes, which are certainly far more interesting than the others. The early ones prove her to have been an active and conscientious worker by day. Now she appears as an equally active observer by night. Till now she had never exhibited in writing this side of her character, though her friends knew it. All the sentences I have printed here are hers, though I have rearranged them in order to bring them into chapters. Because of this, as well as for their richer material, the diaries have now lost the dryly journalière *style to which we were well accustomed at our committee meetings.*

EDITH OLIVIER

Chapter I

MISS NIGHTINGALE IN DERBYSHIRE

For over a year, we lived under the imminent threat of war, and a year is a long time—long enough to make a habit out of expecting something that never happens. The expectation has so far been so much more real than the event. It is like the Day of Judgment. Those people who believe most sincerely in that (and I am one) would yet be astounded if one morning they were awakened by the Last Trump, instead of by the well known and rather irritating barn door cock; or if they looked out of the window to see, instead of the postman on his bicycle, or the milk cart unloading bottles at every door, a light in the top of the sky, overhead an army of angels, and the Great Scene of the Opening of the Books being enacted. Many of us have always believed that this will happen one day; but no one can deny that when it does happen, it will cause some surprise.

With this kind of sceptical belief we continued to think of a war with Germany, throughout the late summer of 1939. All the time, we spoke of it as a possibility: and all the time in our hearts we thought of it as an impossibility. War is so antipathetic to most English people, that it was almost equally antipathetic to believe that any country could desire it. Especially as it seemed that no one in the world would gain anything by it. We had heard the cry of "*wolf*" before, even a year before at Munich; and then Mr. Chamberlain and his umbrella had protected us from the Beast who seemed preparing to spring.

In August I spent a long-anticipated holiday in Derbyshire. I love sight-seeing, and the great houses which I visited had all the historic splendour of my dreams. But about them, there seemed to be something ominous in the air, as if a snowstorm should suddenly sweep across a harvest field. The sheaves would still be standing in their hyles; the greater part of the heavens would still have the brilliant blue of an August day, yet a cloud would have hastened by, portending the coming of another season. It is difficult to explain, for the anxiety was not definite enough to spoil those brilliant days. They were not "*Les beaux jours quand nous étions si malheureux*," but rather *les beaux jours quand nous apercevions de loin le malheur qui attendait*. After all, that might sometimes be rather a cosy feeling.

The historic houses of Derbyshire—Hardwick, Chatsworth—Haddon—seem to be, in St. Paul's words, "not made with hands". All great architecture is like that—having an existence apart from its concrete shape, as it did exist in the architect's mind before the building arose. But these famous houses exist too in virtue of certain people—mostly women—who have lived in them. To Bess of Hardwick we do indeed owe the construction of the wonderful house linked with her name, but even she was no architect. She was a vital, wilful woman, for whom houses were letters written in the only alphabet designed on a scale large enough to express her personality. Even so, she did not write the words with her own hand. She dictated them. Her many houses stand like decrees or ukases issued by an empress.

Dominating manlike woman as she was, Bess of Hardwick did really live in the masterpiece which, in its outward form, expresses her so vividly. Its great galleries speak of the day when queens and duchesses lived in state. Those grand houses were the essential settings for a grandeur which their owners never doffed. Small rooms could not have contained it. Wearing it, they moved through the "daily round" which must make the life of every human being, in all ages and in every state of life. In those splendid days this "daily round" was framed on such a scale that in order to maintain it duly, it called for hoops and ruffs and great jewels, as well as for an accompanying retinue. If Hardwick seems unhomelike today,

8

that is because it was built for people who couldn't have lived in anything smaller; so it cannot be quite a home for men and women who live simply, as the greatest noblemen live to-day.

It demands the duke's train of equerries, and the duchess's group of young ladies practising embroidery under her eye.

Needlework is in many ways the most homely of the Arts; and nowhere can there exist a greater wealth of needlework still in its original place on the walls of a house, than can be seen at Hardwick. Much of it was worked by its famous owner and her still more famous prisoner; but, as they sewed, the Countess and Mary Queen of Scots were surrounded by their households. The households were sewing too. This is why the Great Gallery speaks so clearly of those women of the past. We can almost hear their voices—the capable arrogant Countess, the tragic heart-winning Queen; but the language they speak is foreign to us to-day.

Foreign too, in a way, is the amazing staircase, which seems not to have been built, but to have evolved its own pride and beauty, forcing the stone into life to create it, and then forcing that same stone into immobility to preserve it. Foreign again is the Great Gallery, which in my eyes is the only rival of the Wilton Double Cube, in its claim to be the finest room in England. Each is unique, and in a completely different style. Running round Hardwick Gallery is that wonderful Tudor frieze, alive with actual portraits of the Derbyshire Yeomanry in Queen Elizabeth's day. The figures are in relief and their clothes are brightly painted. Below them hang the famous Hardwick tapestries—not only one set, but several superimposed one over the other. There were too many in the house for them all to be exhibited at once, so they were hung to be shown in succession during the different seasons of the year.

There stands Hardwick, among the coal pits of Derbyshire, speaking the language of an earlier civilisation than ours, going back to beyond the coal pits. Yet it does also belong to the year 1939, because it belongs to the family of its builders. They possess the Hardwick tradition, and though fashions may change, there is an unchanging element in the English aristocracy which continues to give the Cavendishes the natural run of the house.

Nevertheless, at Chatsworth, ordinary people of our generation find it easier to step back into the past. The rooms are equally enormous, but the ghosts who live there are not terrific feudal figures like Bess of Hardwick. They are more human. For me, the Chatsworth ghosts are the eighteenth-century ghosts of Reynolds' day. On the walls are the unforgettable portraits of the two lovely duchesses whom he painted. In the Library are countless letters written by that enchanting family group, which, beside the Devonshires themselves, included Lady Bessborough, Lady Caroline Lamb, Lady Granville, and others among the best letter writers of an age when letter writing was a fashionable art. Within Chatsworth you breathe the atmosphere of those letters.

Life there in the eighteenth century was already growing nearer our own. The grandeur of Bess of Hardwick was a thing of the past. Eighteenth-century duchesses played parlour games; they gambled their fortunes away: they wrote brilliant familiar letters to their friends: we should not find them alien to us.

There is an amusing letter from Lady Bessborough to Lord Granville Leveson Gower, written during one Chatsworth Christmas party, telling him of a "paper" which her niece Harriet had "written out" to amuse the guests. It purported to be "the request from the Duchess to her company". Lady Bessborough goes on, "one of them is begging each Lady to confine herself to twenty volumes at a time, and thanking the Gentlemen for their care of the books, which they kindly abstain from ever opening or looking into at all, least [sic] they should injure them by their studies."

This little joke reaches the heart of any book-loving hostess of today.

Chatsworth is not built on so formal and definite a plan as Hardwick, though its Park is a work of art of another kind. It recalls the French landscapes of the classical period—Poussin, Claude, and the rest; but in England the peak of landscape painting had not yet arrived. Instead, the English *dilettanti* of the time created in their parks actual landscapes, too vast for any canvas. Chatsworth possesses many of these on a magnificent scale. Great sweeps of parkland, ridges, waterfalls, fountains, statues—these are the visual memories one carries away. Also the figure of the Librarian, arranging and rearranging the drawings and letters in the Library, into so many portfolios that throughout the longest life of any one man, there could not possibly be time to look through, much less to catalogue, them.

Haddon Hall belongs to the Duke of Rutland, and its beauty is supremely romantic. It is not on the great scale of Hardwick or of Chatsworth, and the woman with whose name it is for ever associated was no Bess of Hardwick. Haddon was brought into the Manners family by Dorothy Vernon, its lovely heiress who eloped with Sir John Manners in Queen Elizabeth's day. Sir John was already "a young man of great possessions" for he possessed thirty manors, and was called the King of the Peak. The world has forgotten the names of those other thirty, in order to remember more vividly the manor of Haddon, down the steps of which the beautiful Dorothy ran to her lover one moonlit night. These steps are what most people remember best at Haddon Hall, and they are indeed the perfect setting for a romance of which they have continued to tell the story for nearly four hundred years. Personally I remember even more clearly the exquisite walled garden so beautifully laid out, and the Long Gallery with its delicately carved panelling of ashen brown, and its Tudor mural painting, which merges so naturally into its continuation by Rex Whistler. We sat talking in the Gallery for a long time.

The present owners of these houses are none of them over middle age, and, naturally, their children are younger than they. There was a feeling of gay youth in the rooms, although their walls possessed the dignity of age. The Duke and Duchess of Devonshire have not long succeeded, they are a fine and ducal pair. The sheer size of Chatsworth might easily overpower a youthful successor, but the Duchess dominates the place by her grace, her height, her presence, and her beauty. She is also very amusing, a quality one dares not expect in a duchess. The Duke of Rutland might have walked out of the Castle of Otranto, and the Duchess has a delicate spiritual beauty. The younger generation was growing up handsome, happy and debonair. The neighbourhood still rang with the story of Lord

Harringtons coming of age party, when once again all classes in the county had feasted together. It was a continuation of the historic past which lives on in the present in houses like these. Then, suddenly one shrank from the thought of the future. Had we reached the end of a period?

Throughout the month of August various rumours floated about. We talked of them all the time and yet we never really believed them.

"The Duke of Devonshire has gone to London for a meeting of the House of Lords. . . . He has sent for an estate lorry to bring away his valuable pictures from Carlton Gardens. . . . He has had secret intelligence that London will be bombed within the next few days. . . . He has counter-ordered the lorry. . . . Hitler is climbing down. . . ." We clustered round the wireless to hear Mr. Chamberlain's speech in the House of Commons. It never came through. *"The Houses of Parliament have been bombed by a modern Guy Fawkes and at the very moment that the Members arrived."*

After all, we were on the wrong wavelength.

I must confess that all this uncertainty made me uneasy. If there was to be war, I ought to be at home for my A.R.P. work; and once war had broken out, I might not be able to travel. I had my own car, and I determined to go home a week earlier than I had intended. I left early in the morning, being sure that the roads would be blocked by military traffic. I drove from Derbyshire to Wiltshire—a very large slice of England, and in all the way I saw not one single soldier. In peace-time, Salisbury Plain is full of them, but now they had all vanished. What could this mean? Had our troops left the country? There seemed to be more war on the wireless than in the world.

And now I am back in my own bed, where I have written down this record of the past few days. Already my drive of yesterday seems to be a landmark. It lies behind me like a watershed, the rivers flowing from its summit in two directions. On the far side they go to the England of the past, an England which for many centuries has not known war, where the manors, the mills, the farms, and the commons have ever lain serenely around the towns with their cathedrals, their mayors, their factories, and their railway junctions. Even the growth of the great midland towns has left the country unaltered. But on the near side of this watershed, the streams already seem to flow fretfully, uneasily, and uncertainly. Yesterday's drive was over a no-man's-land. It lay between the past and the present and I know not where we are tending.

I am thankful to have had that week in Derbyshire, for I believe that those stately days will never quite come back. The beauty, the history, the happiness, and the pervading sense of a great past brooding over each of those houses—all of these will suffer eclipse at least for a time. Yet those who have known what all this means, will surely be bigger people to face what is to come.

I feel sad when I think of those young people I saw last week. I would be terrible if they were to die without knowing the best this earth can give them: they appear to be born with an innate right to it. I rebel against the idea that they may have to turn their backs on that noble civilisation which their forefathers created, and to strike out into a new world of which tanks and munition factories are the emblems. Still, they may be better able to lead the way into this new world because their fathers were the leaders of England in the past. Anyhow they will not be afraid. They can't be. *Noblesse oblige.* But *I* am afraid, and that makes me feel ashamed. I dread what may be coming, and this shows me that I must be growing old. It would not matter if I were killed by a bomb. I have lived my life, and evidently, from my unease this morning, I shall not be of much more use in the world. Mine is the elderly persons point of view, unable to cope with a world completely unlike the past. But the young will fearlessly face whatever comes and will prove themselves able to meet any unknown tests. Maybe, this is what those of us who survive will see most clearly, and admire most wholeheartedly, in the coming years—the rising generation rising to a task which we know to be beyond ourselves.

Chapter II

THE FIRST COMING OF THE LODGERS

A year or more before the war began, the Government decided that our village was overcrowded. A good many houses were "condemned", and the Council agreed to begin by building fifty new ones. The land was bought. Our plans were made and accepted by the Ministry. The money was borrowed. We posted up in the village shop some drawings of the New Estate as we hoped to see it completed, and we fully expected that it would be lived in in a very few months.

Then came the war. All our plans were stopped, and during that autumn between two and three hundred schoolchildren with their teachers and caretakers had arrived in the place. They were followed by over five hundred soldiers who were to train in the neighbourhood, and we also had the staff of an evacuated ministry. The nurses and doctors of a hospital train now descended upon us and gradually there arrived a number of people who had been bombed out of the large towns. Also many residents in the village invited their London friends to take refuge with them. We were already pronounced to be overcrowded. We had built no new houses. How then were these newcomers to be accommodated?

The answer was "Hospitality".

By the first of September nearly every house in the village was prepared for guests, as the Government had decided to evacuate from the ports and large towns all children whose parents consented. This order was not compulsory, so in the country we could not be sure how many children we might have to receive. We accordingly did our best.

On Friday afternoon a little crowd waited at the school for the first arrivals. This crowd consisted mainly of prospective "Uncles and Aunties" (as the children immediately decided to call their hosts and hostesses) and also of a throng of car owners who had been pressed into service to drive the children to their new homes. We waited for nearly two hours. At intervals, strings of buses appeared at the end of the street. Our hearts leapt with welcome. Cavalcade after cavalcade drove past us, laden with children going farther west. They sang and cheered us as they passed, while we waved to them. They looked very gay, and evidently treated this as an extended "children's country holiday excursion" and as great fun.

At last our line of buses drew up, and out of them stepped about two hundred children with their teachers and caretakers. A certain number of mothers had come on the understanding that they would help the hostesses by mending clothes and by generally caring each for a certain number of children. The space outside the school was now full of a swaying crowd. Its nucleus was the army of newcomers, looking a little confused and lost. The uncles and aunties pressed forward to make friends, and to try to walk off at once with this or that child or family of children, to whom they had taken a fancy. The Chief Billeting Officer sat scribbling at his table, sternly forbidding anyone to remove the smallest scrap of a child, until its name and new home had been registered by him. The general population of the village had by now increased the crowd, for everyone wanted to see what was going on. Among them appeared a curious little party which was at that moment arriving at the place—a platoon belonging to a labour battalion. They were very unlike our previous idea of soldiers, not being composed of vertical lines and curves, like most human beings, but built up of clumsy squares and right-angles. Rather like swastikas. They also stopped to look on.

"Schoolchildren?" said one of them to me, "so this is a safe area."

"It will be, now you soldiers have arrived," I said to him. Whereat he laughed a gorillian laugh and went on his way.

Meanwhile the headmistress of the visiting school was sorting her flock into families, or parties of friends, in order to help the Billeting Officer.

That headmistress was a marvel—a combination (hitherto unknown to me outside French seventeenth-century memoirs) of statesman and Mother Superior. She had not arrived intending merely to control and to teach in her school; but to make sure that, whatever were their new homes, her children should know (and they did know it) that their lasting home was in her large heart and her wise brain. She loved them, planned for them, and never failed them.

This school was a "junior school", all the children being under eleven, and they were a touching little crowd as they stood in the large semicircular entrance to our school. Every child carried in its arms a large bag or bundle containing its luggage, and each had a small package of emergency rations. Slung over every shoulder was a gas mask—then a new sight for us, and because we were not accustomed to it, it seemed all the more horrible that it should be necessary for these tiny children to bear this fresh burden.

For an hour or two, I joined the other car drivers in conveying children to the more distant houses; and at last I returned to find that my own allotted party consisted of three small girls—two sisters, Beryl and Yvonne, and a little friend Rosemary, who was five. The biggest room in my house had been converted into a dormitory, and after a supper of milk and biscuits we soon tucked them up into bed. They knelt down first to say their prayers. They were very winning.

Two hundred more children arrived the following day to be met and allotted to their uncles and aunties in the same manner; and then we were warned to be ready for fifty blind people who had been dispatched to us. It was not easy to find homes suitable for these somewhat difficult guests, but at last we succeeded in finding hostesses for them. We waited for six hours for the blind people to arrive. No sign of them. At ten o'clock we went home, leaving instructions with the police to guide them to the shakedowns which we hastily extemporised for the night in the Village Hall. The policeman promised to telephone to some of us, directly our blind guests arrived. We heard no more of them, but it was rumoured that they had been driven to another place of the same name where even shakedowns were not immediately available.

We grown-up people were accordingly very busy all that Saturday, but whenever I got home for a few minutes, I heard the gay voices of my new family playing games in the garden, supervised by my delightful cook, who turned out to possess a genius for managing children.

On the Sunday we were told to go to the nearest junction, to meet another two hundred children. Here we waited for some hours, while the billeting officers bustled about arranging meals for the seven hundred who were the total number expected, and whom they were to allot to the various villages. Late in the afternoon, we learnt that none of these children were coming, and I never saw better-tempered people than those billeting officers, who had so fruitlessly given up their whole day. Such mistakes were bound to happen during this sudden exodus, unparalleled in all of our minds since the days of the Pharaohs; but in spite of small blunders, many children had been successfully removed from danger. Would that all had reached safety, instead of such numbers remaining, at their parents' wish, in the towns, to be murdered by German bombs.

In the next month or two, the small welfare committee we formed to look after the children, had a very busy time. Naturally, the arrangements made in those hurried hours while the bus loads were arriving, were not all quite suitable; and in the first few months, nearly half the children were moved from one billet to another. This meant much work for our committee and it also was a great bore to the Chief Billeting Officer, who would fain have "let sleeping dogs lie". But we found too often that they were not "sleeping", and would not "lie".

One complication was that a party of mothers and "expectant mothers" whose children were sent here, had been themselves evacuated to another place beginning with the same letter. The authorities had imagined that this alphabetical proximity naturally carried with it a geographical one, but unfortunately this was not the case, and the other village was about twelve miles off. For some days this caused a ferment. First of all, one of the mothers (who farther happened to be "expectant") having been located in this remote spot, arrived at our school screaming for her children who had been sent here. She and her two children made a terrific scene, yelling and shrieking in the school yard, while I tried to explain that as the two places were in different rural districts the exchange must be arranged by the two councils. I promised that this would be done as soon as possible. No good. The yells grew louder. The Chief Billeting Officer, being a stickler for law-abiding, refused to let me take the matter into my own hands. I therefore conveyed the party to his office, where I pointed out to him that, unless we made an exception in this case, the "expectant mother" would soon be "expectant" no longer, and that the alteration in her status might take place in his very office. This changed his opinion, and he delightedly consented to our sending the whole family, as quickly as possible, at least twelve miles away.

The next day I had my hands full with another woman, who had come from Gibraltar with three children committed to her care, and had lost them all. She was billeted in this same remote village with one screaming boy of her own; and hearing that the "expectant mother" of yesterday had been successful here, she arrived demanding that we should now produce her lost ones. We couldn't. We telephoned to every place in the neighbourhood and those children could not be found. I at last committed the party to the care of the W.V.S., who I am sure were more successful.

But on the following day, our welfare committee succeeded in bringing nine mothers from our "opposite number" village to join their children here, and then things became easier.

During those first few weeks school holidays were still going on, and we arranged community games in the Rectory garden for our visitors. It was rather a business to convey my small lodgers to and from these, and we soon saw that when lessons did begin, the children who were billeted on the outskirts would have to be moved nearer the school. Mine among them. In many places, the additional number of children obliged the authorities to arrange that each party should only do half-time lessons, which meant that all the children were running wild for half the day. We were lucky, as we had a couple of small halls which were handed over to the newcomers, and the Rector generously gave up his dining-room as another classroom, so that both our home children and the visitors could have whole-time school. This ensured practically no disturbance to the curriculum of either school.

Then came the day for calling in the children who had been billeted far from the schools. My beloved little girls had to go. They howled when they went, and my cook and I nearly did the same. I could not think how to deal with the situation, until I had the brilliant idea of taking them, *en route* to their new homes, to see a herd of cows being milked by machinery. This made them quite anxious for the moment to come when they could leave my door, and we had a most happy afternoon watching those cows, who did not at all agree with the queueing-up system, but were trying all the time to shoulder each other out of the way and get in first. We then had tea at a little tea-shop in the village and the children seemed cheerful when I parted from them. Later in the evening, my cook found Yvonne in floods of tears, having run into the street trying to make her way back here by herself. And then my dear Mother Superior came to the rescue, consoled the little girl, and the next day she assured me that all my ex-lodgers were "settling down".

The "dormitory" was not long vacant. Two or three days later, I heard from an old friend, whose husband was a General about to take an army to France. She asked me if I could tell her of an hotel where she could stay during the last weeks while he was training his troops in the neighbourhood. I told her that "this house was the only hotel I could recommend"; and in a very short time I had two more children in the dormitory, this time with a nurserymaid sandwiched between them. Kathleen was eight years old, and was a kind elder sister to Victor, who was only five, and young for his age. He seemed more of a baby than the determined

Rosemary, the baby of the last party, though he really was the same age. When I had a tea party with my two sets of lodgers, Victor was the hero of the day. The little girls combined to make much of him, and he adored this.

It was a happiness to me to have this little family in my house. The General was with his troops all day, and in the evening he came to dinner, arriving usually in time to play with his children for a quarter of an hour before they went to bed. After dinner, he had an hour or two with his wife. I knew that these were his last hours before he left for the front, and my one idea was to make myself scarce. Fortunately we were still in the stage (a stage, by the way, which has never ended) of grappling with our Black-out. That horrible effect of Hitler's totalitarian war has at least one effect: it sustains ones wrath against its originator. But in those early days, the black-out served another purpose. It gave my sister-in-law and me an excuse for leaving the husband and wife alone, while we wandered round and round the house for about two hours each evening. No black-out was ever more completely tested and examined; and after the General had left, no German, however strong his Zeiss glasses might be, could have seen a gleam of light from any of my windows. But black-outs are the most temporary things in the world. Two years later, at the beginning of another winter, I made a fresh inspection, and decided that any invaders could sit comfortably in my garden, reading their maps by the light which escaped through the gaps in my once perfect black-out. But those days had not then arrived.

I had some good talks with the General who, although the most reserved of men, was one of those rare people who can be interesting without giving secrets away. One day I asked him whether, in these days of tanks and aeroplanes it was still true to say that, in the last resort, wars are decided by the infantry. He said:

"I still think so. Whatever material damage is done by aeroplanes, however swiftly tanks may get through a given piece of country the last millions of undefeated men, standing on their own feet, will have the last word to say."

Another question which I put to him concerned the Siegfried Line. Would it have a crucial effect on the war? The General said:

"It sounds impregnable, but is only concrete. Its strength depends entirely on who is behind it."

I wrote down these *dicta* in September 1939, leaving time to prove their truth or falsity.

In the Squire's house was billeted a baby "school" for "under fives", who were not often seen in the streets, for their playground was the Park. Every detail of the children's equipment was perfect: their beds, their washbasins, their armchairs, their tables, their desks, their pots, and the pictures on their walls. They were a most friendly party and when I went to see them they crowded up, examining my clothes, opening my bag, and interested in all my belongings. They were like minnows clustering round some strange object that has fallen into the water. Their language was appalling, and a great surprise to us country people; but I often wonder what the effect will be on those slum babies of the memory in after life of those months in one of the famous great houses of England. They had awoken to a new world of beauty, space and peace; and because its outward character was so unlike the streets of Kentish Town, it would surely remain for ever in their minds.

By now we were driven to housing our bombed-out refugees in the houses which before the war had been "condemned"; and in order to furnish them, everybody lent what furniture they could spare. Pieces of carpet were very precious, and, like everyone else, I lent my garden chairs, my picnic tea-sets, and any blankets I could do without; and I gave away all my old clothes. Some of these people were not very welcome. They did not like the country, and obviously did not at all want to settle down among us. Their rooms were the picture of discomfort, though they could not be blamed for this, as the buildings were dilapidated and the furniture was never enough to go round. But they seemed naturally rather like gypsies. If a visitor tapped on the door the whole party opened it, crowding round full of curiosity and peeping out, one behind the other, at every sort of distance from the floor level. In appearance, these people were completely unlike our natives. They seemed foreign, with their narrow faces, their pale skins, and their dabs of lipstick.

Only once in these evacuation weeks did I hear the real sound of a voice which was maddened by panic. It belonged to a London woman who had been in a shelter when a reservoir nearby was bombed, and the shelter was suddenly flooded. She had seen many of her friends drowned in that shelter. Her husband was a soldier quartered somewhere near us, and she had fled here, but when she arrived she could not find him. This unbelievable last straw completely broke her down. She stood in the square outside our Committee Room, and her inhuman shrieks were terrible. I brought her upstairs to our room; and it really did not take us long to find her husband, whose officers were most kind in giving him leave to come to us, but in that short interval she cried most pitiably. It was like no sound I have ever heard. All the time her little boy sat stolidly by, reading the *Pilgrims' Progress*, which he said he had never read before, and thought was a very pretty book. He apparently did not hear his mother's sobs.

I soon found that she had eaten nothing all day, and then I decided that the all-healing cup of tea might meet the case; so I invited her to come with me to our small village tea-shop for a little meal. One of our committee members proved that she was wiser than I. I had merely seen this unhappy woman as an abnormal creature, but she saw deeper. She found the real woman who had been submerged by the flood in that shelter. She knew that this woman would in the past have done her daily housework, cared for her little boy, cooked for her family. My fellow committee member reached that normal woman, and called her back into action. I now saw what was almost like a treatment by artificial respiration.

"Don't you go with Miss Nightingale," she said. "I was just going home to get our luncheon, and I would like you and the little boy to come and have a snack with us. You won't mind helping me to get it ready will you?"

The idea of this little piece of work was the first thing that brought the unhappy woman back to normal. When I went to see them an hour and a half later, she had helped to get the dinner ready, she and the child had enjoyed it, and now she looked serene. Her husband had just gone out to find some lodgings for her, and the immediate trouble was over. Love and wisdom had healed the broken spirit.

Chapter III

NOT FORGETFUL TO ENTERTAIN STRANGERS

In the first few months of the war, one problem faced all of us, who had, either perforce, or of our own free will, become landladies—I mean the problem of amusing our guests. We soon saw that the visitors, mostly people from the towns, found country life very dull; and we saw equally that it was essential to find some occasional outlet for the strangers within our gates. The close quarters were too close.

It began in a very simple way, with the children. During the first few weeks, the evacuated schoolchildren were not sent to school. The arrangements for this were not completed. So that it came about that about three hundred strange children were wandering about the streets, for they were afraid to go farther afield. This question did not take long to settle. Community play solved it, and the Rector's garden. Our own young people were very proud to conduct the guests backwards and forwards, and to teach them the local games; while the visiting teachers and friends kept the whole thing under control. When once the school term had begun, this was no longer necessary; but every kind of person in the village had got some idea of what it meant to give a big party, and to keep that party going. I believe that every village was tackling this job and most of them did it very well; but what struck me about it was that we found ourselves, for the first time, mutually responsible for the happiness and welfare of strangers in our neighbourhood. Automatically everyone was caught in this new activity, and I believe it showed to many people a new, and far more enjoyable, aspect of rural life. Hitherto, visitors from London and other big towns had been the property only of the friends or relations with whom they spent a week or. two in the summer. They seemed to think themselves superior to the rest of the country people; *so* superior in fact that we all had believed in their superiority. Now they appeared pathetic, homeless and at a loose end; and it was our part to "show them round".

This did not apply only to the children. The mothers were even more out of it. They had left their husbands behind, and someone with only a male view of housewifery had decreed that hostess and guest could easily share the kitchen and, still more impossible, the kitchen grate. If two separate meals were to be cooked simultaneously, such meals could easily be "staggered". The word "staggered" in that sense had not hitherto reached our village, but the suggestion was sufficiently staggering in itself, without seeking for any new meaning of the word.

Here then was another appeal to entertain strangers. It too was on a small scale, but it paved the way to more elaborate entertaining later on. It again gave a sense of responsibility, as a place and not as individuals, for making our visitors as happy as possible.

We opened a little afternoon club for mothers and babies. They ran it themselves, and it was a "place of their own". When we went there, we went as guests. We now saw another aspect of entertaining—giving people the opportunity of entertaining themselves. This again increased our social acumen. The club did not last long, as most of those mothers went home in a short time; but it helped us to find our feet in another of the new paths which were opening before us.

As President of the Women's Institute, I now had a new idea. This was to organise two "War-time Banquets" for the members. All the world knows that a *Cup of Tea* is the climax of every well-conducted Institute meeting; but these banquets were to be climaxes of climaxes. To begin with, they were luncheons, taking place before the meeting really began. Their primary object was not conviviality, though it must be admitted that this was a conspicuous by-product of our banquets. They were destined to show us with what excellent meals we could feed our families and friends, without using any ingredient which had been brought overseas, or which, in fact, had required any transport at all. The dishes were made by members from materials produced in the place. We each brought our own plates, knives, forks, and spoons. Also our own glasses. But here the President stepped in. Glasses, yes. But the tumblers used throughout the meal must be filled with water only. At the end of the banquet, when the famous home-made wines which have made the reputation of many of our members, were produced, to drink the one toast of the day—*the soil of our native country*, I made myself responsible for the wine glasses. I produced liqueur glasses; for I knew of old the charm and potency of some of these drinks. I therefore took care that while we drank wisely, we should not drink too well.

We learnt a great deal from these banquets, on the subject of living luxuriously from our own back gardens; although later on Lord Woolton did cold-shoulder the too free use of our poultry yards and our home-cured hams.

But in the first months of the war, we could with clear conscience, enjoy not only the vegetable soups and stews, and the tarts packed with fruits of our own growing, but also the cold chicken and salad and the game pies (made largely of rabbits). How good they all were! But what I personally enjoyed most of all was a dish of Barley Bannocks, eaten with home-made cream cheese. All my life, I had heard of these as the food for pigs, which the labourers' families were reduced to eating in the "hungry forties". A hundred years must have matured this legendary food, for it turned out to be the most delicious kind of hot biscuit, made of barley meal; and I only wish I could often eat it. All the bread at these banquets was made from flour grown on our farms and baked in our own ovens.

We had now become tea-party conscious, and our Institute quickly gave a party for the evacuated mothers with small children, when musical chairs alternated with piano sonatas, and riddles with religious recitations—the whole winding up with Sir Roger de Coverley. It was very lively.

As Christmas drew near I had another and most enjoyable party for some refugees from Vienna and Czecho-Slovakia who had succeeded in escaping to this country before the war began. I had heard that they were homesick for the Christmas trees of their native land, and I decided to decorate a little one for them. It could stand on our tea table, and could afterwards go back with them to the house which had been lent them as a home. Most of them had not yet learnt to speak English fluently, while we none of us knew much German. As for Czech, till that afternoon it had been a dead language to us all. It was therefore to be expected that this party would fall very flat, and that all its sparkle would have to come from the candles on the Christmas tree. Quite the reverse. We learnt that no party is so amusing as one which consists of people who are more or less strangers to each other, and who don't understand one another's language well enough to know at all what anyone else is talking about. This opens the door to the gayest and most unexpected plays on words. It is the latest form of the old game of cross questions and crooked answers.

I suppose it is still necessary for diplomats to know the language of the country to which they are accredited, though I believe that it often happens that they know, or think they know it, too well. Perhaps if two countries were on the verge of breaking off relations, a verbal misunderstanding might be the last straw. But if it is only a case of breaking bread together, these mutually incomprehensible lingoes add sauce to the dish. The most commonplace people become original. Very rapid steps towards intimacy are made, when everyone is teaching his partner how to translate two quite unknown languages into one another.

A feature of this party was that it inspired one of our guests to tell us something about the Christmas customs of her own country. She made an entrancing picture of Vienna as she had known it in Christmas seasons; and it seemed tragic to think that a people of such human sympathies, and such romantic and happy tastes, could have fallen under the harsh and unimaginative yoke of the Nazis.

In the charming account of a Viennese Christmas, we learnt that the Christmas trees do not only stand in the houses, but also in the parks, for the birds too are given their *Christ-baume*, hung with scraps of food, and surrounded all day by the quivering wings of flights of birds swirling round and round and perching for a moment. Every morning fresh food is put out on these birds' Christmas trees, and all through the season, the parks are alive with the twittering, fluttering hosts.

Viennese squares also have their Christmas trees, which appear, brilliantly lit, weeks before the day itself. They are inscribed "*Give to the poor*". Everyone, rich or poor, responds to this appeal as well as he can, by giving presents to the Christmas Committees who arrange that no one shall be left out. Then there are the Christmas markets, open-air stalls which go on for several weeks, laden with cheap presents, and also with little fir trees to be converted on Christmas Eve into family Christmas trees in each home. The Sunday before Christmas is called Golden Sunday, and on that day all the shops remain open, to give people a last chance of buying their presents. On Christmas Eve comes the family supper of coffee. and *Striezl*—a wonderful pastry, plaited with almonds, raisins, and other fruit. Our Viennese lady told us that this tasted "marvellous". And then we heard of the beautiful midnight Mass when the country people walk in from long distances through the night. In a district like the Tyrol, this pilgrimage sometimes takes several hours, often through deep snow. She described the lanterns twinkling one by one as they appeared through the doors of far-off farmhouses on the mountain-sides. You can watch them coming down the hill until they meet each other, to unite in a soft wide stream of light which vanishes at last into the church door.

As we heard all this it seemed that the sacred beauty of the *Weihnachten* must still exist; but alas, it is now a thing of the past.

These little parties were our apprenticeship in the art of entertaining strangers, but bigger things were to follow. The village made friends with the men of a Yeomanry regiment from an adjoining county who had been sent here for training, and we decided to organise a weekly dance for them. One difficulty faced us at the start—how should we find partners in the village to balance this large influx of the male sex? One of the organisers explained to me in some anxiety.

"We haven't got nearly enough loose girls, we must import some."

I am a life member of all the local Moral Improvement Societies for the benefit of the young, and in the name of them all I rose to protest against this importation. I then learnt that the word "loose" related to the proportion of women to men in our village, and had no moral significance. I withdrew my opposition.

We accordingly invited a bus-load of girls from a neighbouring place to give the required balance to our dance, and I watched, with some interest, the arrival of the "loose girls".

They entered in the huddled and close formation of a swarm of bees, and in that formation they seated themselves well apart from the men. Here they murmured together, like the bees which they resembled in appearance. I could not think how we could effect the desired fusion between the two sections of our guests. But I had counted without our Master of the Ceremonies. He was a sergeant-major, with the winged feet of Mercury, the social tact of Beau Nash, and the gift of imparting to the lumpiest partner something of his own grace of movement. With an airy tread he now floated to the middle of the ballroom and called on the gentlemen to *Take their Partners*. If any gentlemen seemed laggard (and many did) he led them to the now well awake and buzzing swarm of loose girls, and made personal introductions. The most alert and attractive of the girls were soon paired off, but there remained a substantial residue who looked heavy. Our Mercury was not deterred. He swung himself into the fray, and danced a few rounds with each of the unpartnered girls. They at once seemed to be the most graceful dancers of all, and as the M.C. relinquished each one in turn, she was at once snapped up by a fresh partner. This mercurial man made all our dances the most brilliant successes.

These dances were interspersed with first-rate concerts which were particularly enjoyable to us amateur landladies for, besides hearing some very good music, we were asked to put up the distinguished artistes who came from London. The first of these concerts might be described as an "All Star" one, and for us country people, it was a new experience to have in our houses those well-known favourites of London audiences. We were extremely proud. Beatrice Lillie proved to be, both on the stage and off, as gay as a lark and most wilfully charming. I had feared that her very sophisticated talent might not go down with these country yeomen, but I could not have been more mistaken. When she stepped on to the stage, and threw round the room one of her most demure glances, she captured the audience without singing or saying a word. They would hardly allow her to begin, much less to leave off, once she had begun. In fact it seemed that she was on the stage for the night. But not even this situation was beyond her. She suddenly spied, in the audience, Miss Gwendoline Brogden, who, in the last war, made a famous hit with her song, *On Sunday I walk out with a Soldier*. Then followed this dialogue:

"What are you doing here, Gwennie?"

"Listening to you, my dear."

"Come on the stage and give us a song."

"I have given up that sort of thing."

There was a little more of this kind of talk, called, I believe, "back-chat", and then Beatrice addressed the room:

"Won't some of you help Miss Brogden up?"

The army rushed into the breach, and Miss Brogden was carried to the platform. Then came a little playing about with the accompanist, and she broke into her *Succès fou* of twenty years back. It went like wildfire.

After the concert, the visiting artistes, with their hosts and hostesses, met some of the officers at a supper party, and, for those of us who were lucky enough to be invited, this was quite as amusing as the entertainment itself. It was like those suppers on the stage which we read of in the days of Beerbohm Tree. And now we were there. No real supper on the stage could have been more enjoyable. The company included opera singers, concert singers, jazz musicians, classical pianists and violin soloists. Amusing speeches were made, and both Beatrice Lillie and Olga Lynn gave some of their Imitations. Everyone was happy.

We were not late in getting home, as these parties for soldiers must always end early; and when we were back in my house, I had an interesting talk with one of my guests, who had been singing English songs at the concert. In peace-time, he was a partner in a firm famous in the world of books, and had music as his recreation. Now he was a private soldier and had carried his love for music into the ranks. I enjoyed hearing him talk about his comrades. He had made many real friends and liked particularly mechanics and the men who practised trades. He said that he found the true yokel was, as a rule, a man without either ambition or ideas; but I believe he would change his mind if he saw these men, as we see them, in their own milieu, on the farms and among the animals. I feel that no industrial worker in these mechanised days can know so much of real life or can see its purpose so clearly as the agriculturalists who, all through the year, work with Nature and watch her processes. Such men probably feel homesick in the army.

Our next concert was given by an A.A. regiment which offered to travel half-way across the South of England to entertain the soldiers in our village. They were practically all professional musicians. The condition was that we should give them beds, and this was rather difficult, as the company was a large one. The Colonel of our regiment said he could arrange it, provided that I could find out beforehand the ranks of the various performers. The list came. It included no less than eighteen "B.diers". I was thoroughly frightened. Was it possible to deal with eighteen musical Brigadiers? The thing was beyond us. I was much consoled to find that the Colonel was not in the least disturbed and said he could easily find beds for the Sergeants, Corporals and *Bombardiers*. Their Colonel stayed with me and acted as accompanist, and this partly explains the musical prowess of the regiment. He was in it heart and soul. The company performed a revue, written, composed and produced by themselves.

Certainly in that first autumn of the war, we could hardly believe that a war was actually going on. The country was doing what it ought to have done before, training troops for what seemed to be some future war; and our only responsibility was to provide comforts and pleasures for these troops.

About Christmas-time we embarked on our most ambitious attempt in military entertainment. This was a pantomime written, produced and played by local amateurs with a little professional help. It turned out a great success, which was surprising, as it fell a victim, in succession, to every contretemps which is supposed to befall amateur theatricals.

First of all, the company looked on rehearsals as rather an amusing way of spending an hour or two, if there was nothing better to do. The accompanist alone never failed. She accompanied with a complete efficiency, whether or not there was anyone to accompany. Those members of the cast who did sometimes appear, immediately settled themselves in remote corners of the room, there to finish the secret conversations which had begun outside. When the producer succeeded in luring them from these retreats, nearly everyone had first of all to explain, that he or she was not that day playing his or her own part, but was "reading" for an absentee. The patience of the producer proved that this virtue is a supernatural gift of the spirit; but on the one occaasion when it did break down, the terror he spread among his flock, and their subsequent good behaviour (which lasted more than one day) proved that he ought really to have been in a fury all the time.

Even when the first night arrived, we found that the whole company had never before met on the stage. And on that occasion, our Pantomime Queen was "down" with an attack of laryngitis which eventually seized, in turns, practically the whole company.

Terrific quarrels developed behind the scenes. Some of the performers had to be coaxed on to the stage in a manner which I believe is sometimes adopted with performing dogs—by holding out a biscuit to create the dramatic bound from the wings. Our "biscuits" were extremely complimentary remarks which we said we had overheard in the audience about the acting of this or that player who had considered himself slighted on the stage. The feuds which now began, were declared by the participators to be eternally incurable, though I believe they were forgotten as soon as the pantomime ended.

Yet none of this drama was guessed at by the spectators; and from the other side of the footlights the whole thing looked rollicking fun. But during those strenuous weeks I saw why it was that one of the most successful theatrical entertainments of my youth had been called "*A Pantomime Rehearsal*".

Our pantomime was not only played for our own regiment, but it travelled to all the neighbouring camps, and then was played under the patronage of the mayors of several seaside resorts, at last actually reaching London. Indeed its run lasted until nearly Easter. I did not go with it on tour, as my part was a small one and a substitute could easily be found.

As time went on, we found that the troops were far more capable of entertaining themselves than we were of entertaining them. It transpired that among the men quartered in our neighbourhood were members of some of England's most famous orchestras, and also a member of the Committee of the London Philharmonic Society. He set the ball rolling and there began a series of brilliant symphony concerts, some of which were held in a gymnasium capable of holding over two thousand people. This was far too small for the crowds of music lovers in the army who pressed to hear the programmes put before them by the artistes. Remembering this, it is irritating to be told that the very inferior music often produced in the B.B.C. Forces' Programme, is chosen because this second-rate music is the only kind which soldiers will tolerate. I should like those who say this, to have been compelled to stand among the hundreds of disappointed music lovers, time after time, who were left outside in one of the coldest camps in the country when the "House Full" notice was posted over the Symphony Concert Hall. But no doubt these programme makers would not have thought our concerts worth queueing up for, especially with the chance of being left out in the cold after all.

After these concerts, we natives were always asked again to show hospitality to the soloists who had been good enough to come from London to take part. Virtue was indeed its own reward. For one thing, being a hostess, I was allowed a seat in the concert hall, which was practically impossible for the ordinary civilian. And then, the music over, we always had in my house a small supper party for the visiting musicians and the concert organisers. As I looked round the table, it always seemed to me like some very grand supper party on the stage at Covent Garden, and I am sure that its gaiety and spirit equalled those. Among my guests on various occasions were Dame Myra Hess, Dr. Malcolm Sargent, Jelly d'Aranyi, Adila Fachiri, Harriet Cohen, May Harrison, Dennis Noble, Edythe Baker, Cyril Smith, Denise Lassimonne, Nancy Loder and many more. These famous musicians were always ready to offer their gifts to help in concerts for the troops, and they made us feel that the whole thing was a festive occasion for themselves as well as for their audiences. They certainly were festive occasions for the landlady who had the pleasure of entertaining them.

At this time, rationing was not as yet very stringent; though, as the months passed, it became more and more difficult to put before our guests the good food they deserved. But they themselves always brought "the feast of reason and the flow of soul", and these delicacies have not even yet been rationed by Lord Woolton.

Chapter IV

NO MORE QUIET NIGHTS

My London visitors have always remarked that this is a very quiet house. From their point of view, I am sure they are right, for I look upon London as distinctly a noisy place. But they go on saying this even now, since the war began; and when they arrive out of the world, they do not at first perceive how much the house has changed in the past two or three years. I expect we are still quieter than an engine-room in an aircraft factory; but from my point of view, the nights now are full of unaccustomed noises. I hear many sounds from my bedroom which I did not hear before.

In the past, there were certain night sounds to which I was completely accustomed, and which I loved very much. There was the perpetual murmur of the water streaming through the weir, a few hundred feet away. It is the place where old Mrs. Andrews, who drove the carrier's cart, was drowned about sixty years ago; and since that long-distant night, no other unexpected sound has been recorded, as breaking the peace of the river, flowing under the bridge on its way to the sea. Another almost continuous sound was made by the wind in the trees, but this was not often disturbing, for we have few storms in our valley, and the rustle was seldom more than "a little noiseless noise amidst the leaves". Then there were the intermittent noises—the cries of the water birds, the hoots of the white owls, and sometimes the harsh voice of a startled pheasant, though nowadays that familiar voice brings a new message, for if a bomb falls within many miles of us, the pheasants feel the earth's vibrations long before any sound reaches us. The first we know of it, is the clamour that the pheasants make, as they argue with one another about it. Then we used to hear a cow mooing for her calf, carried away that morning to market; and quite seldom a wandering cat called outside.

Now we think that our nights are distinctly noisy, and they remind us that even here, in the depths of the country, we are at war.

When the Germans raided the Midlands—Coventry, Birmingham, and other industrial towns—all through the night, we were being taught (as we never had been taught before) that, geographically, we were on the direct air route from Berlin to the English Black Country. Then came nights when the Royal Air Force was, in its turn, on the way to Germany or to Northern France. A like roar was over us till morning. Sometimes again the planes we heard were flying round about to protect us, but I have never been able to discriminate between the sounds made by our own aeroplanes and those of the enemy. To me they sound equally diabolical.

On other nights, a convoy of tanks or military lorries passes through the lane. These convoys can truly be said to make night hideous, and it is quite impossible to sleep while they go by. Between me and the road are a lawn, a shrubbery, and a high wall, but these cannot deaden the noise of the convoy; and the din of battle made by totalitarian war even penetrates, night after night, into this remote and peaceful park. I believe that the word "*Park*" and "*Paradise*" have the same origin, and this was formerly easy to believe. Now it seems that our paradise has been invaded, not by one devil in the silent slippery disguise of a serpent; but by the whole Hosts of Satan for

> "Clamour such as heard in heav'n till now
> Was never; arms on armour clashing bray'd
> Horrible discord, and the madding wheels
> Of brazen chariots rag'd; dire was the noise."

That is what a tank regiment sounds like as it passes down a country lane.

Beside these, my bedroom is now invaded by lesser, and less horrible sounds; though equally unfamiliar. They also are due to the war, and they are made by my lodgers. To me they are often most extraordinary.

Till now, I have preserved a virginal innocence as to the noises men make at night, and now they strike on my ear as surprising. In all my homes, I have succeeded in securing for myself a bedroom cut off from the rest of the house, and this is the case to-day. There is a dressing-room between me and the stairs and passage, and through this space, no sound can pass. A guest going late to bed has never disturbed me. Then, when I agreed to have an officer billeted on me, I gave him the ground-floor room directly beneath my own. So for the first time, I have had a succession of near neighbours, and masculine ones at that. I find that men cough, sneeze, and clear their throats, more than women do. Many snore, though this is not so universal as I imagined. They also throw their weight about till the bed creaks beneath them. They open and shut boxes, drawers, and cupboards. Over and above these general male tricks, each man has his own idiosyncracies; and these are magnified at night, when everybody, man or woman, thinks that solitude sets him free to behave as he likes. By day, I have grown very fond of each of my lodgers in turn; but at night, as I hear them hurling themselves about their room, I am glad that they are not my husbands.

An early tenant was a famous fisherman; and during the summer, when our clock time was two hours ahead of the sun, he seemed to copy the Twelve Apostles and to "toil all the night", though, unlike them, he did not end by "taking nothing". Some time after midnight, when we had been long in bed, I used to hear him returning in his waders—squish-squash—squish-squash—over the lawn and under the colonnade. When he reached this point, he tugged off his boots, and dropped them one by one on the pavement. Then to the kitchen, to collect the largest dish in the house, which was to hold the largest fish ever seen. When as children, we learnt to read in our spelling books about "*A Fish on a Dish*", we never imagined anything so enormous as this. So thought the lodger. And he felt that we ought to know more of fishes on dishes than we had learnt at the infants' school. Now he walked round the house, like "Wee Willie Winkie", tapping on the doors and crying at the locks to ask if he might come in to show us his catch. We sprang from our slumbers to see him holding before our sleep-ridden eyes, eight or nine enormous trout or grayling, dripping with silver water from the chalk stream, and gazing at us with their blank, dead, opaque eyes. It always seemed that this must be a dream, until these fish appeared again next morning, grilled for breakfast, or lurking in lettuce as a mayonnaise for luncheon.

Another lodger was a bad sleeper, and he groaned piteously in the night, waking with really terrifying cries of anguish which lasted till he could bear it no more. Then he got up, and, to my relief, I heard the kindly pop of a bottle of beer. This, and a meat lozenge, had a very soothing effect, and both he and I generally had quiet nights after this treatment. When I spoke of this to another of my lodgers he at once recited what he called a "Potted Biography". It was this:

"Mr. Alfred Beit
Screamed suddenly in the night.
When they asked him why,
He made no reply."

I never heard these lines before, though the lodger said they were a well-known classic. I cannot say that they contain much beauty, though I don't deny that they were appropriate. I admit that they prove that the suffering lodger was following in the footsteps of other famous men, but the cause of his groans is made no clearer. The whole episode confirmed my conviction that, as a race, Men are Mysteries.

A very congenial lodger was the one who sat up till the small hours of the morning, deciphering old family records for a book he meant to write. At first I found it quite impossible to go to bed when he was here, but sat listening to letter after letter, dating from the middle of the eighteenth century to the beginning of the twentieth. And from such enchanting people too. Five or six separate books could be written from those papers, and I wish I were clever enough to write one of them myself. Such reading aloud is the kind of night noise to which I was already more or less accustomed; and I enjoy it more than anything, even though it means sitting up later than is my custom. It completely satisfies the soul.

With this cultivated young man I had an amusing adventure, late one night, when our literary labours were over. Staying in the house at the time, was a well-known literary critic who enjoyed, as much as we did, the delving into ancient history which gave our evenings so much glamour. An hour or two after we had gone to bed, cries for help came from the young historian. The household assembled in his room in an indescribable mixture of night attire—myself, the critic, and my two maids, for this was before young women had been called up to join the services. A tap had broken, and streams of water were pouring from the fixed basin into the bedroom. We all turned out to be completely helpless. Nobody knew where to find the main water control of the house. This, I may remark, is one of the pieces of "General Knowledge" which Hitler has since forced us all to learn; but in those early days, none of us had traced our water supply back to its source. We clustered round the overflowing basin, armed with all the futile tools we could discover. And here I must confess that, in pre-war days, I had never tried to play the part of the female "Carpenter Brother". I was, and am, no mechanic. Nor were any of the others. We tried to tighten up the tap: it retaliated by ejecting a succession of sharp bursts of water into our faces. We tried a more soothing method, swathing the tap in piles of towels, but they were quickly saturated, and the water dribbled through them on to the floor. At last, in despair, we surrounded the danger spot with baths, into which the water rattled with a continuous clatter. Then we all bolted, taking with us the bed and bedding, with the awakened sleeper. All were transferred to an empty room, and thus we awaited the morning.

One of my lodgers made his first appearance in the house some time after midnight. His luggage had already arrived, with a message saying he would come "after dinner"; but when ten-thirty had come and gone, and there was no sign of his appearance, I declared that I didn't mind whether or not he had lost his way and fallen into the water. I refused to drag the river at that hour in the night. However, some time after I had gone to bed, I heard a brisk step approach the house, followed by some uncertain movements within it. I knew that the lights were out, and I guessed that the lodger was groping for the switch. I pulled myself together, and went downstairs to receive, with my most conventional smile, a young man whose beauty made me dizzy. He was exactly like a Guardsman in a "*Ouida*" novel. With courtesy and some diffidence, he explained that he had been kept late at the office, and had lost his way in the wood. With equal courtesy, and a certain modesty, I showed him his way about the house, and then went to bed, to hear his voice, in the room below, keeping up a continuous flow till morning. At first I thought he was saying his prayers. Then I decided that he must be reading poetry aloud. Though either sound was a little disturbing, I rejoiced to know that a young gentleman of so much physical beauty also possessed these elevated tastes. The next morning, he hoped that he had not disturbed me by "using the telephone".

The explanation was that, as a Staff Officer, my new lodger had a private telephone installed near his bed, by which he nightly passed the secrets of His Majesty's army.

This officer was an ardent soldier, and he soon decided that the work he was temporarily doing in the office would not keep him in condition for active service. He therefore made up his mind to sleep out of doors, and as he could not be parted from his telephone, every night he put his bed within reach of it in the colonnade under my window. Here, instead of interrupting the quiet of my night, he helped to preserve it. It was a very wet season, and nightly, the rain thundered down upon the pavement below me, so that sleep was really often impossible. But this young man was one of those healthy youths, whose slumbers nothing can break. He lay, like a quieting carpet between the stone paving and the water-spout, which kept crashing from the sky; and as he did this, he broke for me the din of the downpour. On one particular night, I had to warn him, before he went to bed, that the rain was too much for him to face; and I ordered him to sleep indoors. He disobeyed. At five in the morning I heard a scrambling sound outside. I looked, and behold, there was my lodger suddenly springing awake, and rushing indoors like a gigantic piece of animated and saturated sponge. Water streamed from every yard of him. Next morning, the house looked as if Niagara had flowed through it in the night. I censured the lodger for this childish escapade, and sentenced him to a school-boy's punishment. He had to write out a hundred lines:

Miss Emma Nightingale is always right.

I now had a very tall lodger. He looked about seven feet high, and, probably because of this, he seemed to be rather ill and sad. His one consolation was music, and I believe it was the reputation of my piano which brought him to the house. He played upon it till one o'clock every morning, but this did not keep us awake, as he was far away from any of our bedrooms. When at one time, he could not use the music-room, he migrated elsewhere, and another lodger, not knowing that he had changed his room, thought she heard him extemporising an opera in the dining-room. This did not surprise her, as she believed that no form of music was beyond him; but next morning she found that, failing the piano, he was consoling himself with the wireless.

He also telephoned a good deal during that part of the twenty-four hours which, before the dawn of the Electric Age, could truthfully be called "the stilly night". This epithet is now everywhere out of date.

My latest lodger was rather a disappointment, as he moved about the house as quietly as a mouse, making no sounds by which he could be identified. One evening I thought I had caught him out. He had gone to bed early with a cold, and some time later on, a sudden succession of metallic crashes resounded through the house. A lady lodger hastened to my room saying in agitated tones.

"Did you hear that noise; I believe the Major has fainted. Oughtn't we to go downstairs and see what we can do?"

My housekeeper was passing the door at the moment. She looked in and said:

"It was only the casserole fell off the frigidaire. That's all."

Casserole and frigidaire represent extremes of heat and cold, so their clash would doubtless create most unusual results; but I had not guessed that the sound of a Major fainting was so equally extraordinary, that it could be mistaken for a casserole falling off a frigidaire.

However, the Major could clear himself. He was, after all, innocent of any connection with this sudden sound in the night.

Chapter V

UNIFORM OR UNIFORMED

It is perhaps natural to treat these two words as having an almost identical meaning, but, none the less, it would be to-day a natural mistake. Hitherto, I have lived very little among soldiers, but now I am surrounded by khaki; and the appearance of all these men, going hither and thither on their unfathomable business—their faces drilled to the same expression, and their figures adapted to the same uniform, at first creates the impression that this uniformity must extend to the mind.

Before the war, all the soldiers we met were what we now call "regular soldiers", and in those days, I believe our impression would not have been far from the truth. Soldiers were as apart from the world as monks and nuns, though they would never have admitted it. Their minds, their speech, and their lives were drilled into a pattern. Unconventionality was "bad form", and only a man of outstanding character could save himself from adopting a rather dull conformity with the majority of those around him. If life were to be looked upon as a gigantic game of General Post, a young officer joining a line regiment in peace-time, might be pardoned if he concluded that his own call to play would inevitably come when the Postmaster announced: *"The post goes from Sandhurst to Cheltenham"*. For was it not towards Cheltenham that most retired Colonels and Majors gravitated, there to spend their declining years? More than a touch of genius was required to throw off the weight of routine which culminated in this predestined goal; and only that same touch of genius could lead a man to the top of his profession.

I am an old country woman with no right to possess, or to express, any opinion about the army, especially as I knew so little about it till the war had changed its character. But looking at it from outside, it seems to me that, pleasant as the regimental system must be for men actually in regiments, who find it as cosy and friendly as a good club, yet it must tend to narrow the outlook. It is a hard test of mental independence, to be doomed to spend the whole of one's life, from twenty years old onward, with the same group of about thirty men, especially as, to begin with, they are all one's superior officers. Sailors are different. They serve in ship after ship. Their allegiance is to the Navy as a whole. Their experience includes service in all manner of crafts, and with all manner of men. Nearly every man in the Navy seems, at one time or another, to have been "shipmates" with nearly every other man in the Navy.

But the army of to-day is different from the army of yesterday. The "regular soldiers" are greatly outnumbered; but though the newcomers, do their best to look as uniform as possible, yet, sooner or later, one finds, under the khaki, the old friend unchanged and unspoilt. This is very admirable. Here is a generation of men, belonging by race and environment to the most individualistic nation under Heaven, and who, from the day they left school, have lived in a world of complete Go-as-you-please. Now, of their own free will, they are merging their separate personalities into membership of a profession with ancient and inviolable traditions. The point is that they have *merged themselves*. They have not been *submerged*. The verb is active, not passive.

So when my house became a point of halt for a succession of army lodgers ("billets" they call them), I found that the new army might indeed be uniformed, as it was, but it was certainly far from Uniform. These are no uniform men. They are uniformed Barristers, Stockbrokers, Artists, Journalists, Schoolmasters, Business Men, Country Gentlemen, Agriculturalists, Professors, or Literary Men,

It is indeed true to say of the British Army which is fighting Hitler, that it is a cross section of the nation as a whole.

I think of one officer who came here and whom I had known previously as an outstanding man of science. At first I could not find him when I went to meet him at the station.

There seemed to be no scientists about. Brisk and businesslike, a martial stream of men issued from the platform, their faces sternly set on the quickest route for the only two station taxis. From their speed, an onlooker might have supposed that they had been shot out of guns. Then suddenly I recognised my man. He too seemed imbued with Purpose. He had lost all appearance of the scholar, and, instead "a Trainband Captain eke was he".

And even when I thought I had recognised him, I still had to make the acquaintance of this soldierly fellow. So completely had he adjusted the outer man to the new career, that I felt we should have to begin all over again. But I soon learnt that the Doctor had never thought of doffing the Scientist before donning the Captains uniform. He had carried into the Army the scientific knowledge of a lifetime; and his army experiences had been absorbed, not by the mentality of a junior officer, but by the critical and constructive mind of a trained man of science. He was now uniformed: that was how he came to march so swiftly towards the taxi rank. He was still the original thinker: that was why he was going to be of special value to the Army.

When the Russo-Finnish war was drawing to its close, this Doctor had been sent on a mission to Finland, to investigate health conditions in the country. Finland is very sparsely populated. What we should call a hamlet, they call a village; and their towns, are the size of our villages. The Finnish Army was then in the act of retreating before the Russians, and the Doctor knew that it would bring with it a large number of wounded, who must be cared for in these tiny villages. He told the people that a Field Hospital must somehow be extemporised, but this was something quite outside their experience. They made him tell them exactly what its purpose would be; and then he learnt the practical and self-reliant character of this primitive people. They had no central organisation to fall back upon. They had no guidance except from an ex-army sergeant. But within two days, with seemingly no materials at all, they turned a disused old factory building into a hospital, which actually did receive over a thousand cases. They pressed into service anything which they found under their hands. The wood from old sleighs, and broken farm implements made an operating theatre, operating tables, stretchers, surgical splints, and stands for operating lamps; while the lamps themselves were made from old electric bulbs rejuvenated. The whole thing was a miracle of improvisation.

The Doctor then watched the evacuation of the Karelian Peninsula. This began as a unorganised movement of a whole population; before the advance of enemy troops, and later on all the world saw in France, what a disaster such a thing could be. Here, the refugees never became a rabble. As they arrived, each village received and retained that proportion of the passing stream of people which it could absorb in suitable and necessary employment. The others went on to be received elsewhere in the same way.

"How could this possibly be carried out by untrained peoples?" I asked. "Here, with no enemy in the country, we had to use several Government departments to tackle that job. And even they made some mistakes," I concluded, thinking ruefully of our lost blind people.

He shrugged his shoulders, as if he had no explanation to offer, but what he said was something like this:

"They were like a colony of white ants. The communal mind seems to act when each individual has his own special job set before him, and realises the purpose of *that*. And, too, there must be enough self-reliance to act without waiting for instructions. When a high individual development and a high degree of communal spirit coincide, then an entire people moves. That national genius constantly came to the surface in Finland, whether it was in manual work, in civilian administration, or in such a case as that of the solitary soldier on guard, who scared a whole Russian detachment into retreat by pretending to be a ghost on skis."

The Doctor found in our own country an equal efficiency in small groups, like members of Fire Services, Home Guards, or isolated platoons. He was specially struck by a Fire Service in a port where he was acting as Medical Officer early in the war. They responded to every demand, as if they had been for many years a trained brigade, and then he was surprised to find that they had only been training for a few months. They created their own organisation to meet their own needs. The Doctor said he had found that such is the way in which human beings will behave, if their individual, their professional, and their community lives are so regulated as to depend upon the responsibility of the individual. He was so strongly convinced of this that when he was invalided a few months later, he planned and founded an industrial and farming community in the form of a training college, which was attached to a well-known aircraft factory. I have seen this at work, and it seems likely to become the pattern for a society which would fulfil every human capacity—spiritual, intellectual, and practical. And this was my first experience of the difference between uniform and uniformed in the Army of to-day.

Another officer who came to my house had been for many years in the Middle East, and he seemed to know it, not as one "knows the palm of one's hand", but as a child knows a sand castle which he has built up from its foundations on the sea-shore. He was a quiet, unobtrusive man, and it was a real surprise to find that he had, for many years, been on easy terms with Noah, Abraham, and Melchizedek—not to mention Arabs of every rank and occupation in Egypt and Mesopotamia during the past twenty years. As the child knows the sand castle, so he knew that part of the world, for he was a famous archaeologist, and his knowledge of the past was gained by digging into its foundations in the company of hundreds of Arabs of the present day. He knew their dialects perfectly, and therefore he knew a great deal about the men who spoke them; for a dialect is, of all speech, the nearest to the thought of the speaker. Dialect and slang. Those who converse in either of these open their thoughts in a way which no trained speaker can ever do. His verbal currency has passed through too many minds.

This man had actually dug into Noah's Flood, and what did he find there to-day? Eleven feet of seemingly undisturbed earth, lying between layers of ruined cities, each of which represented one of the successive civilisations which the world has forgotten. In those primitive lands where many races have come and gone, the digger generally finds the ruins of many cities one above the other, each one mingling with that immediately before or after it. But here, in the heart of Mesopotamia, when one particular city had been excavated, the excavators came upon those feet of apparently virgin soil. A less experienced digger would have thought he had come to the end of what the site would yield. Not so this one. He dug on, seeking another world hidden below that anonymous stratum and then he found that he had come to the remains of the antediluvian world where, "in the days of Noe, they did eat, they drank, they married wives, they were given in marriage, until the day that Noe entered into the ark, and the Flood came, and destroyed them all".

Now the scene of all those banquets, those wedding feasts, those gay and reckless festivals, and those royal palaces, where the men lived who mocked at Noah as he built his ridiculous craft, and drove into it his motley flocks and herds—all of these have shrunken into eleven feet of mud.

Quoting from a book in which he himself has described this, discovery this learned seer said:

"Below the deposit of sand left by the Flood we found two beads of amazonite, a green stone for which the nearest known source is in the Nilghiri hills of Central India, or in the mountains beyond Lake Baikal—and at once there is called up the astonishing picture of antediluvian man engaged in a commerce which sent its caravans across a thousand miles of mountain and desert from the Mesopotamian valley into the heart of India."

I watched the face of my lodger as he told me about this. His eyes seemed to scan the history of the human race, as calmly as if he were watching a child play with its Noah's Ark; and then I thought that one's sense of proportion must be greatly changed by an experience dating from before the Flood.

Many architects are now in the Army, and several came to my house. One in particular had been known to me before, for he had designed the group of council houses which we were planning before the war, and now, instead, he was designing accommodation for A.T.S. Not with the amenities, I presume, that he would have provided for us, because the Army did not give him such a free hand as we had done. I realised this, when I appealed to him in vain on behalf of a company of girls in which I was interested, who were living in a camp not far away. They were accommodated in some out of date "Married Quarters". If they wanted a bath, they were obliged to draw their water from an outside well; then they boiled it in the copper; then they carried it upstairs. They now asked for permission to have their baths in the kitchen where they cooked for the regiment to which they had been allotted; and where every day they were surrounded by an unlimited flow of hot water. This permission was refused, as it was evidently feared that the poor girls might be tempted to wash in the soup which they were sending up for the men. Their officer then tried to get the concession of having one day a week reserved for the A.T.S., in the fine large bath house lately built for the troops a few yards away. The answer was that this would necessitate a watch being put on to the bath house during the whole of that day. Army Orders did not allow for this. It was indeed a case of: "Water, water everywhere and not a drop to—"—wash in.

However, my friend the architect had no voice in the question of where he should build his bath houses, or for whom they should be built. His one responsibility was for their actual construction. I thought he was being wasted.

Working in the same office was another architect, who had considerable experience of Town-planning on a large scale, and he delighted us all by telling us that he considered our village to be a perfect example of Planning. We immediately saw that he was without doubt a man of great taste, and we invited him to give us a lantern lecture starting from that text. Unfortunately, during the course of this, the lecturer went on to remark on certain flaws which later generations had allowed to creep into the original plan. We then changed our minds, and agreed that he had no taste at all. The general opinion was that *we know what we like, and there's the end of it.* This frame of mind is not unusual, and many schemes for building a new England will founder on this rock when the war is over.

Another architect who appeared in uniform in my house, was one who had designed a church in an adjoining county, which I had much admired, during a pre-war sightseeing tour. His special job in the Army seemed to be teaching languages—an odd thing for an architect to be doing, except on the assumption that the architectural profession dates back to the Tower of Babel. In character he reminded me of Mr. Darcy in *Pride and Prejudice*; and this not only made him an amusing and witty guest, but I feel sure must have greatly increased his powers of keeping discipline in his class.

And then there was the painter torn from his easel to view the landscape from a tank and to discover an unexpected new beauty in the world as he watched the dawn rise over a column of these monstrous black engines of war, after a dark night spent in a wood during manœuvres. But he did not altogether desert his easel, for he spent many a half-day's leave sketching, and I now possess, among my mementoes of the war, an almost complete series of paintings by him of my house from every possible point of the compass. His brother officers must have enjoyed having among them this rare creature, who decorated their Mess Room with caricatures of them all in the guise of Roman Legionaries; and whose portrait of the regimental cook was the envy of the Sergeants' Mess.

One of my early lodgers was a Cambridge Don, who seemed always to have possessed at least one war-like taste, as for years he had studied and collected old weapons. When he gave the army of to-day, a lecture on Tanks, he traced these back to the Long Bows which won the day for the English Archers at the Battle of Agin-court. As he was a University tutor in English literature, we were always trying to floor him over identifying quotations, and we only succeeded once, when an A.T. beat him on the post. When he went on manœuvres he was inspired to write poetry when he looked upon the landscape with its many memories of fighting from the days of Ancient Britain; and he gained similar inspiration from the famous old house in which his office was temporarily placed.

He was a man of over six feet high and proportionately broad, so I found him rather a handful one day, when a F.A.N.Y. suddenly laid him in my arms in a fainting condition. She had driven him back from an operation at the dentist's, and then fled, guessing that his weight would be beyond her. It was also beyond me; but I resolved to put this F.A.N.Y. into her place by showing her what could be done in time of war by a representative of my own supposedly fragile generation. I hoisted the prostrate figure in my arms and carried it into the house where I laid it on the lodger's bed.

It was rather surprising to find that a tutor from the severely scientific University of Cambridge should also have seen many a ghost as he walked through the Park, but this is probably explained by the fact that he was an Irishman before he became a Cambridge Don.

So the Uniformed men, who have stayed in my house during the war, have turned out to be in no way uniform. I think they were no worse soldiers for that, and, during the years which are to come, it will be extremely interesting to see what they and the Army mutually make of each other.

Chapter VI

A GENTLEMAN EVERY TIME

As I think over my lady lodgers, summing up my thoughts about them, I naturally set them against the background of professional opinion; for, quite early in my career as an amateur landlady, I asked a neighbour who has taken lodgers ever since her husband died some fifteen years ago, whether she preferred ladies or gentlemen.

"*A gentleman every time*" was her prompt reply, and I find that this opinion is shared by most professional landladies. In my case, the decision has seldom been in my hands. I accept whoever is sent to me, and I keep an open mind. If I allow myself to think too much about the weaknesses which lodgers, like the rest of us, are bound to possess, those weaknesses gain strength. They grow until one can see nothing else.

If I say that my lady lodgers have generally stayed longer than the gentlemen, that proves nothing; for their movements are determined from above, and those who stay the longest would possibly have fain gone first.

For a short time, I had the pleasure of giving a home to two mistresses from our evacuated school. I loved these guests. I have seldom met anyone who more clearly gave one the sense of Vocation that did the headmistress. Hers was what is called a "junior school" and all the children were under eleven years old. It used to be thought that anyone could teach the little children, and the really trained teachers should be reserved for the elder ones. The education authorities have now realised that the opposite is the case. Far more imagination is required from teachers of small children, but given that imagination, the mistress of a junior school is much to be envied. There is more skill in the technique of teaching small children, and if the foundations of knowledge are not assimilated before a child is eleven, they will never be assimilated at all. This too is the period when the love of learning is born. I believe it was Sir Robert Peel who said that everything he had learnt of any value in his life, was taught him by his nurserymaid; and there is no doubt that the success of every senior school greatly depends on the schools from which their pupils come.

This lodger of mine was, as I have said, like a character from one of the broad-minded convent schools in seventeenth-century France. While she was with me, her responsibilities were great. The school was accommodated in three separate buildings, so the actual arrangement of the classes was a complicated business. She turned it into an advantage. When the children moved to a new classroom for a new subject, they had to run for some way out of doors, and I often watched the way in which they enjoyed this little break, though it must have been a troublesome matter for the headmistress and her staff. That staff worked wonderfully together, and they treated each other like the members of an Oxford Common Room.

But the headmistress's work was not only educational. The children had come away from their parents and were living in strange homes, but these homes were as familiar to the headmistress as they were to the children themselves. She made friends with the foster-parents, understood their difficulties, discussed sympathetically with them the characters of the children in their houses, and was a living centre of all those scattered groups.

Then she had great responsibilities in the place whence she had come. She remained working under the Educational Authority of her own county, and she was in constant touch with the parents left at home. Her mind might well have been confused among all these conflicting ties; but I never had a more calm and collected companion than this remarkable woman when we met in the evenings in my sitting-room when her day's work was done. I regretted her departure very much, but like everybody else, she was under orders, and they recalled her to tackle the difficult job of returning to her home town to reopen the school there, with reduced numbers of pupils and staff and with the continual danger of bombing.

Rather a difficult job was the billeting in our village of the nurses attached to an Ambulance train, which had to be always ready to remove patients from bombed hospitals, and to convey them to places of safety. What added to our difficulties was that, at the same time, the War Office was seeking billets in the village, and that the Ministries involved had not agreed upon an equal rate of pay. One paid a guinea a week for a gentleman's lodging, the other gave the same price for ladies who had to be boarded as well. No wonder that landladies more than ever preferred "a gentleman every time". It really was tipping the scales unfairly.

We sent a deputation to London begging the Ministry to allow us to put the nurses into a sleeping coach in the train, but we were refused on the double plea of comfort and discipline. Those of us who were on the spot saw that both must break down on very wet nights, when the train sometimes returned at two in the morning after a seventeen-hour journey, to find a furious storm going on. The girls funked the long walk to their lodgings in such weather, and they preferred to spend the rest of the night in the train on bare iron stretchers. Meantime, one landlady at least was pacing her house in great anxiety, fearing that some evil had happened unto them. There was a doctor and his wife in charge of the train and they were very charming and friendly people. He was hard put to it in filling up the hours for the nurses during the many days when, fortunately, the train was not sent off on "operational" journeys. The phrase, "spit and polish" got a new meaning in those smart little wards; and during the months they were here, the nurses beautifully embroidered the name of their unit on many hundreds of blankets and linen articles.

Most of my military lodgers were gentlemen, for, as a rule, the members of the women's Service were lodged in hostels, but for many months I did have a most charming A.T. in my house. She worked in an office nearby and liked it so much that she had to call upon all the strength of her patriotism when she was ordered to accept a commission. She had loved the practical work and the feeling that she was actually releasing a man for fighting.

But the authorities were right in insisting that more officers should be commissioned. The Corps had grown so immensely since it was first instituted that it was completely under-staffed with officers, and the results of promoting the best of the rank and file has amply justified the determination of the authorities.

But in those early days, the A.T.S., who issued from their rough and ready sleeping places were nevertheless extremely smart—shoes and buttons polished, hair permed, lips a solid bar of lipstick. And they were immensely patriotic. At this time they were all volunteers, and they never grumbled at their hard conditions, realising that these inconveniences were due to the Corps being raised so quickly to do such important work.

For much too short a time, I had as a lodger a very lovely young actress, who was recovering from a serious illness, and whose poet husband (now in the Army) was quartered a few miles away. The marriage of this romantic pair is the one memory of radiant unmixed happiness which stands out in the first fortnight of the war. They were married in Salisbury Cathedral, and the family wedding party was a very august one, consisting entirely of Bishops, Generals, Poets, Sculptors, Painters, Writers, Fellows of Colleges, and Curators of Museums.

Then, beneath the soaring arches of the most Heavenward of English cathedrals, and into the presence of this assemblage of distinguished people, the bride had appeared, floating up that long reach of nave, like a spirit form. Her wedding dress seemed to be made of pale mist; and upon this diaphanous material there was indicated a faint pattern of human hands from which escaped a dove of Peace. Her face spoke dazzled wonder, as though, in this dark week of the world's history, she hardly dared to be so happy. Those who looked on shared her feeling, though lacking the power to express it with a like beauty. But I still remember the half-hour beginning with that bride's apparition, as one of the times in my life when I saw, brought into being, the promise of which one dreams in every lovely dawn of the world.

And now, nearly three years later, this bride was my lodger. Could any landlady be more fortunate than to find that the war had brought to her door, as well as the expected khaki figures, social workers, or bombed-out babies, this exquisite being from the land of play acting? With so magic a suppliant pleading for shelter at her door, not even the most professional of landladies could have held out for "a gentleman every time".

Like many of our wartime visitors, this lodger had lost her home by fire, though, strangely enough, not through an attack by enemy raiders. She had been "resting" with her baby in a remote country cottage lent her by her parents, when the God of Fire descended upon it of his own volition. This fragile creature had gone to her bedroom late one night, to find it filled with smoke, and the baby seemingly unconscious in its cradle. She took it in her arms, and ran with it into the garden, where the air soon counteracted the effects of the smoke. The firemen were quickly on the spot, as indeed they usually are, even in the depths of the country, now that every man is ready to defend his own town or village. The baby's mother took a hand with the hose, and they worked successfully at keeping the fire down, till they were faced with a new and unforeseen horror. The water was exhausted. There was nothing left to do, but to let the house go, and to concentrate on saving what was possible of its contents. The actress-turned-firewoman began with her parents' belongings; and this dutiful, though perilous, undertaking prevented her from saving her own wedding presents, or her husband's manuscripts. This adventure had resulted in an attack of rheumatism, from which she came to me to recruit. When the doctor first arrived to see her, I warned him to look for her carefully in her bed, as she had shrunk to the size of a slim stem of bamboo, and he might possibly overlook her.

The poet-husband came to spend most of the evenings with her, and, in spite of her vigorous protests, to push her about in an invalid chair. We made the best of having an actress in the house, by a great deal of reading aloud in the evening; so, once again, I had lodgers who fitted perfectly into my ideal pattern of life. But every morning, the husband distracted me by starting *almost* too late for the workman's bus by which he had to travel in order to reach his camp for early parade. I suffer badly from Train Fever, Bus Fever, Boat Fever, and every other kind of transport fever; but I notice that poets and painters invariably catch trains, however late they leave for the station. I conclude that Providence, proverbially kind to drunken men, is equally considerate towards men intoxicated by the Muses.

As the months of the war went on, my household became stabilised with three or four permanent women occupants, over and above the male lodgers. The first of these was a lady who combined great natural beauty with a mastery of all its accessory arts. She had rather an eighteenth-century appearance—hair *poudrée* (or rather, not *poudrée*, but naturally of a very beautiful white). Her skin was dazzling in colour and texture, and her lips were perfectly made up. Her nails too were touched with a lovely rose colour. As for her clothes, they were *sans reproche*—expensive materials, of faultless design, and beautifully cut. She knew how to put them on, and also how to hang them in her cupboard, so that they should last well and look *soignée* (she liked that word) when she put them on. None of this is surprising when it is added that this lady was a fashionable London dressmaker.

I made her my Mistress of the Robes, and she tried to teach me how to wear my (less beautiful) clothes as well as she wore hers. But I was a wretched pupil, and could never do it right. Her patience in handling this unsatisfactory apprentice was quite unbounded, and it was very ill repaid; but she went on hoping to the end, and her long deferred hope never made her kind heart sick. She continued to inspire me with the belief that I had possibilities.

This beautiful creature must have found country life very trying after her London world, but she bravely made the best of it. Till she came to me, she had never walked alone in the dark, and had been quite convinced that a taxi was the only natural mode of progression for a human being. Now she works in a canteen, and at first she thought that to walk home at night was about the most frightening thing she had ever attempted. She who had fearlessly faced irate producers, spoilt leading ladies, and dissatisfied chorus girls, could not check the beating of her heart when a startled pheasant crowed suddenly as he flew out of a tree on the road home. She who had designed and made wedding dresses and Court gowns to stand up to the criticism of aristocratic mothers and grandmothers, now had to grope her way along a winding path in a shrubbery, with a river gleaming and vanishing almost under her feet. In a few months, she became as brave as a lion in meeting these dangers. Still more, from the first she was quite fearless in facing what was always beyond me, self-satisfied shopmen. She spent hours every week in tackling rations, points, and controlled prices.

She was very critical of people, and expected that, like good clothes, they should follow the fashion of the day. She judged them as types rather than individuals, and she was as often wrong as right. But in one thing she was never wrong, and always right, this was the brewing of cocktails, which she made brilliantly, whether or not she had anything to make them of, and as the war went on, this was not unusual. She may have been driven to use the ingredients which the mayor of a neighbouring town told us he suspected he had made the first cocktail he ever tasted. As a telegraph boy had been carrying congratulatory telegrams to the squire's house after a family wedding. The butler gave him something with which to drink the bride's health. The telegraph boy could only think it was a mixture of Jeyes' Fluid and Stephens' Ink, and I am sure that my lodger often had little better from which to concoct her much-sought-after drinks.

Another permanent addition to my household was a soldier's wife who came as housekeeper, bringing with her a little girl of just under a year old. Margaret Joan was the strongest character in the house. Her mother's recipe for child education was *Love without Discipline*, and the baby ruled us all. When she was told to do anything, she paid no attention at all, but went on her gay way as if she was deaf. She could be most charming, but if she saw another child receive any attention, she yelled for hours. When, by some occult intuition, she surmised that I was having a dinner party, so that her mother would be busy, she refused to sleep at all, but screamed until someone went to sit by her. This sometimes went on for hours, which was not good for the delicious dishes her mother could make in normal times. Margaret Joan was extremely clever; she forgot nothing she had ever heard, and no one she had ever seen. By the time she was three, her vocabulary was larger than mine, or, at any rate, it included many words the meaning of which I did not know. She chattered away about "*twerpy*" people, or "*attaboy*"; and when she was going for a walk she waved her hand and said "*Orrivor*". She sat for hours banging away on a tiny toy piano, singing at the top of her voice "*Jerusalem*", or "*While Shepherds Watched*". She announced the meals from the age of two, and from that time onward she took her part in dusting and cleaning the house, though she did these things in her own way.

The baby was indeed a war-time baby, though fortunately the wail of sirens was the nearest she got to air raids. A siren at once made her mother relegate Margaret Joan to a seat on a cushion under a table or under the stairs; and we all pretended that this was a most amusing game. But you never could throw dust into her eyes. They were too wide open for that, and wide open too for long after she should have been in bed.

If Margaret Joan had not thrown her into the shade, we should have thought her mother was a very clever woman; but like the rest of the household, she had to take a back seat when her daughter was about. She was the quickest person I ever knew, and could produce a perfectly cooked dinner hardly half an hour after she had been singing lullabies to the baby for nearly two hours. Cradle songs are now out of fashion, and the modern nurse has no use for them; but it always pleased me to hear that crooning primeval sound come softly through the bedroom door, though I confess my appetite cheered up when at last it was succeeded by the merry clatter of saucepans and frying-pans.

Both the lady dressmaker and the housekeeper thought more

quickly than their tongue could keep up with their brains. It was therefore often difficult for a slow-brained person like myself to interpret the phrases which I noticed they both used in common: "What's a name—bits and pieces—when all's said and done—this, that and the other—you know what I mean." How are people clever enough to carry on a conversation composed solely of these idioms.

Another familiar of the house was a delightful character, Tilly, the daily woman. She had escaped from a heavily bombed town some miles away, and had been evacuated to our village. She possessed a husband, and a tribe of children, grandchildren, sons-in-law, daughters-in-law, and stepchildren. In spite of this galaxy of descendants, she was still a tall, slim, good-looking woman, with a dignified carriage, and a masterly hand with a broom or in a wash tub. She also had a masterly hand at cards, and won many prizes at the village whist drives, while, once a week, she enjoyed an evening in the village bar. Most of her children had gone with their schools to other villages, and she and her husband made the best of it in the lodgings allotted to them here.

As one watched her face, it was easy to see that, in spite of her youthful carriage, and her power of tackling hard work, she must have had behind her a terrible experience. I learnt what this was when I had to attend a meeting in her home town, and offered to drive her there to see some of her old friends. The place was ruined beyond recognition. We stopped in the middle of the street where her own house had formerly stood. It was gone, so were its neighbours. I left her standing there, looking round with puzzled eyes for some landmark to recall the past and to help her to find the friends she had left behind. She was lost in the once familiar spot.

Chapter VII

SHOPPING BAG AND QUEUE

The first time I remember seeing a queue I did not call it by the now familiar name, nor did anyone else, but I now know that some time in the 'eighties I watched a primitive food queue.

As a little girl, I went to stay with an uncle and aunt who had a house on the Welsh border, and while I was there, they gave one or two big dinner parties. By the time such functions began in my own home, the nursery party was safely in bed; but my playmate cousin was a year or two older than I, and as she was allowed to stay up and see the guests arrive, I sat up too. It seemed to me to be a very grand dinner party, as we sat with Mademoiselle in a comer watching these beautifully dressed ladies and gentlemen talking together about things we knew nothing of. Then Duckfield the butler opened the door and announced, DINNER. As if by heaven-sent inspiration, all the guests seemed at once to know with whom they must pair themselves, and, being paired, in what order they should proceed towards the dining-room. But on this occasion there was one lady too many, and so my aunt decreed that the unpaired lady should be the daughter of the house. She was a tall and handsome girl, and she now placed herself exactly in the middle of the procession. She wore a dress of rose-coloured satin with a very long train, which isolated her from the couple following her, and she moved with an air of solitary and splendid indifference. It is a picture I have never forgotten. I heard Madamoiselle talking in a rather grown-up way to my cousin (who was at least nine years old) about "*la belle queue de Mlle Isobel*", and so the scene has always remained in my memory centred round that word—a word which I did not then know might describe the whole procession.

Of late years, the custom of forming this queue at dinner parties has been abandoned, rather to the inconvenience of the guests. We now pass to our meals in a manner of one of those companies of birds or beasts described by Mr. Joseph Strutt, in his book, *Sports and Pastimes of the People of England*, such as "a herd of crane, a dopping of sheldrakes, a gaggle of geese, a muster of peacocks, a bevy of quails, a covey of partridges, a congregation of plovers, a flight of doves, a walk of snipes, a brood of hens, a murmuration of starlings, a host of sparrows, a charm of goldfinches, a pride of lions, a sounder of wild swine, a dryft of tame swine, a rag of colts, a pace of asses, a baren of mules, a sculk of foxes, a flock of sheep, a clowder of cats, or a shrewdness of apes".

These clowders, bevies, dryfts, and gaggles are shepherded into the dining-room with some labour by the hosts and hostesses, but they often make a bad block when they leave it. No one now has that inspired sense of precedence which seemed to "spring eternal in the human breast" when I was young; and which to-day is limited to the compilers of Debrett and other peerages now too expensive for anyone to buy.

Though there are now few dinner parties, the queue flourishes in the streets and roads. The community has rightly perceived that congregations and gaggles, musters and murmurations, broods and bevies, if permitted on the public way, would inconvenience and hold up the traffic; so in all centres of population, the queue has, in the past few years, been a recognised thing. It is still more or less a new fashion in the country, but now it has arrived, we are beginning to learn its rigours. By all the Laws of the Medes and Persians, a queue is unbreakable, although to the naked eye it does seem to be composed of individuals. But a deadly electric wire runs through these separate units, and anyone pushing through this invisible connecting link, is in danger (metaphorically) of receiving an electric shock.

Those of us who have been accustomed to visiting London, are, of course, familiar with the well-known pre-war queues—the station queue, and the theatre queue; but hitherto we country people have treated them rather casually. Of course, if you think about it, you can't buy railway tickets in any other way than in a queue—though I do remember that, some years ago, I was leaving London by a main-line station, and I ran rather late into the booking office. I vaguely saw a lot of people standing about, and, being a country cousin, I mistook them for a gaggle instead of a queue. Most of them seemed to have stationed themselves quite a long way from the guichet, and as I was in a hurry, I went as near to it as possible. A friend of mine, who was queueing up in the proper manner, as a law-abiding citizen should, was one of those before whom I cut in; but, knowing my country ways, he was merely mildly amused. He afterwards told me with what fury my innocent back was apostrophised by the line of people behind me. This only lasted a few seconds, for I suddenly perceived that I had come to the wrong railway terminus, and I flitted from the booking office in as unceremonious a way as I had flirted in.

I should never do that now, for, in these war days, railway queues are something that cannot be treated lightly. There are queues to admit you to the platform. There are queues to permit you to hire a taxi as you leave it. Docile people accordingly arrive at the station at least half an hour before the train comes in; and they stand patiently, baggage in hand, for all that time, before they can get into the train. On the other hand, people who are not docile, arrive later than ever. They miss the queue, but not the train. They run down the platform, leap in anywhere as the doors are being banged; and though they may have to stand the whole way, so do some of the docile waiters. On the other hand, if you must go by taxi, you can't avoid a taxi queue. The policeman sees to that; and if you want to avoid *him*, you must go by Tube.

Theatre queues have a long and honourable pedigree. I think they must have existed in Shakespeare's day, and that, as well as holding horses outside the Globe, he kept a place in many a queue for one of the courtiers who were afterwards supposed to have written his plays—Essex, or Southampton, or even for Mr. W. H.

of the Sonnets. Theatre queues have always been highbrow. You have only to look at them from without, to realise that. Their members are very superior. They know each other very well and are often as talkative as a literary club. They fill up the hours on their camp-stools with quite good dramatic criticism. Members of queues are really the most alive section of that London public which makes or mars the success of a play; and in that, too, they prove their long pedigree. They descend from the crowd which stood in an Elizabethan pit. Before the war, as they sat on their camp-stools, they ate chocolate, read evening papers, and perhaps studied large tomes about Psychology, Aesthetics, or Economics. I am told that in these strenuous days, you can even meet a Cabinet Minister, or a member of the House of Lords, or of the Bishop's Bench, spending his few hours of recreation in a cinema queue; but I myself have never been in a queue so august as that.

In the country, most queues are strictly utilitarian. They are food queues or bus queues. In fact, there are two phrases which will be for ever inscribed on the hearts of war-time housekeepers—Shopping Bag and Food Queue. Lord Woolton has decreed that "man shall not live by bread alone", but I think he favours woman living by the Queue and the Shopping Bag. For it is no use getting into a food queue, or into a bus queue which will land you in one, unless you possess a shopping bag. Without that, you must carry home a miscellaneous collection of onions, cabbages, fish, and tea cakes in your pockets, for the salvage minister will not let you have any paper.

So every woman now owns a shopping bag, and she is jealously possessive about it. At first, these bags were brilliant and striking-looking objects—in vivid colours and jazz designs; but as the war years roll on, and cleaning materials grow hard to come by, they all decline to the same level of dusty duskiness, reminiscent of two colours fashionable in my youth—Elephant's Breath and Desert Sand.

On the morning when the ration cards for the new week come into effect, there is often a certain amount of well-mannered altercation as to whether or not a landlady and lodger may each borrow the other's bag. The winner of this friendly debate now hangs it on her arm, draws on a rather sorry-looking pair of Wellington boots, and sallies forth to shop. Other housekeepers are doing the same. The first two meet with cordial greetings, and proceed together up the road, talking about food. Another be-bagged figure is now seen approaching. The greetings become less cordial; and indeed they die away altogether, as it becomes clear that quite a number of women are on the same quest. They all hope to catch the early-morning bus to the market town.

Then begins the first queue. It is a bus queue, and queues of that breed are usually very friendly, but not so this early one. It stirs some of the evil passions of the human heart, for it is plainly about to develop into a food queue. Everyone wants to travel by this bus, so as to arrive in time to give its passengers the first pick of the market stalls, and there may not be seats for all. It is all very well for people who live at the extreme limit of the bus journey. There is certain to be room for them. But at every village on the road a little group is waiting by the post office. At first these groups are easily absorbed, but as the bus gets nearer the town, every cubic inch of space has been filled up, till there is no hope at all for people like ourselves, who live only a mile or two from the market. At last the bus appears round the corner. Futile umbrellas hail it, though these are obviously unnecessary, as the driver can plainly see the little crowd which now sways uncertainly into the road. He quickens his pace, and the bus rattles heartlessly by.

This common misfortune draws the rebuffed travellers together. They will no longer be rivals in that first picking over of the market stalls, so they have lost the angry sensation of a food queue, and are merely a defeated bus queue. They consult together. The tough ones resolve to make the best of it, and to walk. Others give up altogether and walk home; while the remaining few form themselves into a gaggle to gossip in the shelter till the next bus comes, an hour later.

The talk last Monday was mostly about coupons. One middle-aged woman, with a thin, practical face, and a badly cut dress, disclosing all the flaws in her shapeless figure, declaimed on the extravagance of buying "Ready Mades".

"Such shoddy material!" she said shrilly. "I would be ashamed to put it on my back. It has gone into rags before you can turn round in it, as the saying is. I buy good stuff by the yard and make it up at home. I made this dress myself," she finished, looking round upon the party with venomous superiority.

The rest of the gaggle looked her up and down, as if to say, "We thought as much". But no one answered.

"I do think it is a shame," said a motherly woman with a little girl at her side, "that we have to give coupons for pocket handkerchiefs. They write up everywhere that

Coughs and sneezes
Spread diseases

and don't I know they do. Half the children at school haven't got a handkerchief, and they splash about everywhere. This poor little one comes back every week with a fresh cold. Well, I've made up my mind. I don't send this child any more, and if the school attendance officer comes round, I shall just tell him off."

The gaggle here broke into two parries, one recommending black-currant juice for a cold, and the other condoling with a war-time landlady, who had lost her best bath towel, which one of her lodgers had taken out bathing.

"And I have to give up my own clothes coupons to get a new one," she lamented. "I shall go naked if they go on like this."

Those members of the queue who reached town at last, hastily separated, and everyone attached herself to one or other of the food queues which were by now in full session—(perhaps I should say in full stance). Queues concentrate on unrationed foods, for if you have a coupon, you are certain of your allowance at any time during the week. And a food queue is an unfriendly thing. People don't talk to their neighbours unless they are anyhow a party. Their minds are wholly concentrated on fish, cakes, or liver sausages—past, present, and to come. The queue moves very slowly and in complete silence, except that now and then a snatch of talk comes from two people who happen to be colleagues and not rivals.

"They 'ad jam rolls. Splendid jam rolls they was too."

"Well, I always say, we may as well 'ave the best."

This came from a most dilapidated woman who looked as if she could not possibly have any idea of what the best, or worst, might be.

Going home by bus, it is wise to start from the bus station, where there is more chance of getting a seat. The station is a spacious square, and buses leave from it for many destinations, starting apparently quite fortuitously. To the newcomer, queues seem to be forming themselves anywhere, and they begin with a vacuum, so it is almost impossible to know on what particular square yard one should begin, in order to catch a particular bus. Then it is very hard to know which is the head, and which is the tail of the queue, and one is pretty certain to place oneself at the wrong end. But these bus queues are very friendly. Everybody seems to know that there will be room for all, and the only question is who will get on first. Everyone helps the other, handing up dogs, parcels, bags, baskets, and portmanteaux, and inviting any lonely person to share a seat. They will tell the stranger where to change, and point out round which corner the next bus can be found. They will even take your part if you get into difficulties through your own folly, and this has happened to me. Not long ago, I was on my way to an important meeting at the far end of the county, and found that I must change buses in a town which was comparatively strange to me. When we arrived, the queue for my next bus already stretched almost the whole length of the street, and I dutifully took my place at its back. When the bus did come, more than half of us were left behind, and of course I was among the unlucky ones. It meant another hour's wait, and when the bus at last arrived, we learnt that before we could take our seats, it must go to a village in the opposite direction, there to set down and to take up passengers. At this there was a movement of rebellion from behind; and a group of officers decided to make this extra journey, so as to be sure of a place when the bus returned. I joined in this advance, but was not allowed to get into the bus, as the conductor decreed that anyone taking this unfair advantage would be turned out on return, and sent to the very back of the queue. The bold officers who had led the advance were not deterred. They jumped in. I hesitated, and was lost. Off went the bus, leaving me like a lost soul floating on the border of Limbo, for I had forfeited my place in the queue, and now belonged nowhere. I was in despair, for I knew I must now miss my engagement. But then a charming little group of soldiers among whose places in the queue I now found myself, invited me to slip in among them. They promised to smuggle me into the bus when it got back, and they did—among their packs and bundles. But for them, I should have been in the road all night.

Once one has edged one's way into a bus, one's fellow passengers are mostly ready to take a part in entertaining the party with gossip and good stories. A bus ride then becomes quite a pleasant journey. It may be rather shaky, but it is far less noisy than one expects; and if you travel on the upper deck, you get quite a new view of the country. It is amusing to look over people's garden walls, and a journey along a quite familiar road can, in these circumstances, become a voyage of discovery.

Chapter VIII

PIN MONEY FOR FARMERS' WIVES

Early in this century, I managed for some years a branch of the National Poultry Organisation Society. Its objects were to encourage the production of eggs in country villages, and to assist cottagers and smallholders to send them to market. There was, in those days, loose in the land, a species of shark called a "higgler", who used to descend upon the houses of innocent villagers and carry off, for a ridiculously small price, the eggs laid by their equally innocent hens. Twenty eggs for sixpence was not unusual, but the poultry grower had no alternative. Owing to the lack of transport, he could not send his eggs to a better market; and if he did not take what was offered, his goods soon became unsaleable.

When I was asked to undertake this work in my own neighbourhood, I at first refused, saying that I hated hens so much that I could not join a society which would bring me into contact with them. Whereupon the friends who were asking for my help promised that I should never see a hen; and in spite of this, within a month I was judging at a poultry show.

It is true that this was outside the ordinary routine of my work, and I think that I was only invited as a "compliment", to flatter my pride in the high position I had now assumed in the poultry world. As a rule, I did see more of eggs than of hens, and, in fact, I gained considerable inside knowledge of the egg trade, so that, when the Ministry of Food began to tackle it, I knew I could have told them a lot.

Nevertheless, I am still prejudiced against hens; and the more I know of them, the more convinced I am that I have always been right in thinking them brainless, immoral, dirty, and hysterical. As characters, there, is nothing at all to be said for them; though it must be admitted they have their uses. Contact with the human race may have demoralised them, as contact with civilisation is said to demoralise the happy amoral natives of some of the South Sea islands. I am told that, if left to themselves, cocks and hens will continue to lay eggs enough to perpetuate their race; but we have diverted their products for our own purposes, and in so doing, we may have induced in them some of the vices of an industrialised society. They have reciprocated this, and, in turn, they demoralise their exploiters; for I have noticed that the most high-minded and honest of my friends are not averse from a little quiet cheating where eggs are concerned.

I won't say more about the unfair promise by which I was inveigled into the Poultry Society, and which led me straight to that poultry show, but I still remember the fall of a lady, whom I have always admired as a shining light of the British aristocracy, as well as of the poultry world. All eggs were sold by our society under the strictest guarantees of freshness and quality, and this lady one day paid a surprise visit to her depot to watch the packing process. She found the manager washing eggs in a dark-brown solution which was new to her as a poultry farmer.

"What is that?" she asked.

"Coffee, m'lady," was the reply, with rather a guilty look.

"Coffee?" she repeated puzzled. "Why coffee?"

"We have got a very good order for brown eggs," the manager now explained.

And how did my friend react to this insidious temptation? She decided that the eggs, in the houses of these pernickety customers, would doubtless make their appearance with the breakfast coffee, so they could not possibly be harmed by a preliminary introduction to the same beverage before leaving the depot. But would she so have fallen if she had not already entered the immoral world ruled by cocks and hens?

I cannot believe it, and, realising the moral risks which we so obviously run in exposing ourselves to contamination by these dangerous dwellers in our backyards, I am strengthened in my views about hens. My friends sometimes say to me, in the self-righteous tones which suggest a practical knowledge of hen-coops, demanding an awe-stricken respect, "Of course you ought to keep a few hens in your backyard". Then such fury rises in my breast that it is all I can do to preserve, outwardly, my accustomed inane expression of gentle good humour.

Not long ago, I much enjoyed a railway journey to London in the same carriage with some City men, who appeared to be so very important that there was no doubt that they must have been "City Magnates". On their way, they fell to discussing this egg controversy. They had all fallen into the snare. Egged on by their wives, they had bought pullets at prodigious prices, in the sure and certain hope of prodigious results. Each wife had met someone playing bridge, who knew someone, who knew someone else, who lived entirely on the produce of two or three hens. These, in turn, lived entirely on the crumbs which fell from these (presumably) rich mens tables. The crumbs had obviously fallen from the remains of the diet of eggs laid by those same two or three hens. I wondered if this was a "vicious circle"; and with my prejudiced ideas on the subject of the morality of hens, I was inclined to think so.

Now the magnates discussed their Backyard Balance Sheets. Each of them boasted that they had had some eggs for breakfast. Yes. Certainly. Some. None at all between October and January, of course. No one could expect that, but quite a nice little lot in March. In fact, one of them had, during that month, "laid down" some twenty-two eggs for winter consumption, as well as feasting on pancakes on Shrove Tuesday.

Now they proceeded to translate this balance sheet into cash. It was less satisfactory. Rather more than one shilling per egg, over and above an unspecified amount of unpaid labour. One of the wives had been cunning enough to make a few extra slices of toast for breakfast every morning, and these added appreciably to the "house scraps", as well as adding some of the grit required to keep the hens in condition. The magnates were amused. They laughed a lot, and agreed that they had made a fine contribution to the war effort.

A surly old man, who, throughout this conversation, had seemed entirely absorbed in the *Financial Times*, now spoke for the first time.

"Better have put the money into War Loan," he snarled; and I should have agreed with him, if he hadn't spoken in such a cross voice.

But the magnates had not made me change my opinion. They were rich, and could afford to laugh at the price of their eggs. I know indeed that one must give the lodgers something for breakfast, and no one can be more delighted than I, if that something is occasionally a new-laid egg presented to me by a friendly neighbour, who has been sporting enough to take the risk involved in those backyard hens. For it is a risk. Who can deny it; Before buying the very small but essential allowance of grain required to make those hens lay, you must hand over your coupons for "Shell Eggs". And if your hens are lazy, and won't lay the calculated number of eggs, your gamble is a dead loss.

To return to my personal experience of the poultry world, I shall always be glad that I ran that Society, as it brought me into closer touch with farmers than with hens. There is no comparison between the two. I vote for farmers every time. They are a most human and delightful race, and I am thankful to know that many of them have been my friends from that day to this.

In those old days, few farmers were really interested in poultry. Most of those who were, generally concentrated on special breeds and sold sittings of eggs, at prodigious prices, for breeding, not for eating. The common or garden hens which snatched and scratched their living in the rickyards, were looked upon as the hobby of the womenkind, and any profit from them was "Pin money for Farmers' Wives". If, however, I were a farmer's wife in these days of the second World War, I think I should change my opinion as to the best way of obtaining eggs. I could escape that gamble with coupons, and leave my hens to scratch for themselves in the farmyard.

But even when, by fair means or foul, you have escaped the

many pitfalls which lie in the pathway of him who would fain walk honestly among eggs, shell eggs, dried eggs, egg powder, and egg-producing foods, and when you have succeeded in enticing the long-desired "new-laids" out of those tricky hens of yours—even then you are not out of the wood. Unless you eat them all yourself, those eggs must be disposed of "according to the regulations". This is really as difficult as getting an egg laid in the first place. Some time ago, I went with a farmer friend to see his poultry farm. In the packing-room was the henwife, a dear old lady who had been for many years in charge of the poultry at this place. She was what would now be called old-fashioned, for she had been brought up to know the difference between a "new-laid" and an "election" egg. She now sat weeping amid stacks of those well-known egg-boxes which each hold twelve dozen eggs, and which, in old days, would have made her glow with pride.

"They're all full," she said, "and the Government won't take them away. That bottom row was put there three weeks ago. And the next row, a fortnight. These 'ere on top are last week's. But they won't collect 'em till next week, and we 'ad such a name for our new-laids. And they take 'em all together—the new-laids with month-olds. Why, we never saw an egg of that age on this farm. It breaks my very 'eart, it do."

"It's a case of the lowest common denominator," said the farmer grimly. "Our best eggs go to market jumbled up with the cookers. Those of us who had a reputation to lose in the poultry market would rather get rid of the whole lot. I shall soon come to that. Most of my friends have."

Now I believe that no Government regulation is entirely unreasonable, or, at any rate, that none is quite illogical. But, on the other hand, I have always thought that logic itself is the most unreasonable of all branches of knowledge. Apparently, you cannot convict a logician of illogicality, if his conclusions can be legitimately drawn from his premise. But what if the premise is false? Logicians make no answer here, and leave Dean Swift with the best of the argument:

"Her foe's conclusions were not sound,
From premisses erroneous brought."

And in spite of the most effective weapons used by the opposition at election meetings, I shall never believe that you are sure to reach a sound conclusion if you start with a rotten egg.

But, after all, it is unfair to say that the policy which has resulted in the diminution of our poultry stocks, begins with a rotten egg, though it may end in one. The reason for the embargo on poultry food is that the weight of grain to be imported in order to keep the fowls alive, is greater than the weight of food which can be expected from them. If this is so, I think that a flock of poultry should be treated like a pack of hounds. Only a few should be allowed to live, to be bred from in happier times.

I suppose it is because people are so afraid of breaking the regulations that we now hear nothing of the tricks, which were practised in my poultry days, for deceiving the hens into laying more eggs. There was one system which banked on the brainlessness of the hens, as being stronger in them than the ordinary laws of reproduction. The birds were kept in darkened pens, which, about three times a day, were brilliantly illuminated by a light from the east. The hens were always taken in by this "phantom of false morning", and, with one consent, they fled clucking to their nests, there to produce a new-laid egg three times a day. Poultry-keepers who can demonstrate their success in this Maskelyne and Cooke deception, might certainly be considered to have qualified for a substantial ration of poultry food, for the produce of their pens must always bring them out on the right side of the Great Grain Gamble.

Chapter IX

THE RISING GENERATION

I remember thinking, when the war began, that, however incapable we older people might be of dealing with the future which was opening before the world (or rather closing down upon it), yet I felt sure that the rising generation would rise to it. I believe this more than ever now, for I had a party to-day which has shown me how courageously they react to circumstances, such as few people of my age ever had to face.

My younger lodgers, and various other young people, had met, more or less fortuitously, in my garden; and, as young people have done in all generations, they at once found that they spoke the same language, and that they had plenty to say in it. No one in the party appeared to be over thirty; and as I listened to their talk, which sounded light on the surface, there seemed to be an undercurrent in it, making them unlike the young people whom I remember in my youth. It is not until now, when, in the silence of my own room, I think over the afternoon, that I realise what it was which they possessed in common, making them like visitors from another planet when I compare them with my own contemporaries.

Each one of those boys and girls knew what it meant to step quickly into a boat, with enemies close at hand, and then to push off, leaving everything behind.

In my day, such things only happened in adventure stories in the *Boys' Own Paper*, but now they appear to be everyday occurrences in most parts of the world. Holland, France, Norway, and the coasts of North Africa—from one or other of these widely separated points on the map, these young people had now descended into my garden. Far from them all was any idea of telling a Traveller's Tale. Their talk was light and easy; yet kindred memories lurked beneath each light-hearted exterior, and now I tried to piece together some fragments which floated to the surface, from each of the half-told stories which I overheard.

There was one enchanting girl who had never before been in my house, though I had often seen her as a *première danseuse* in the ballet at Sadler's Wells. Her figure was of that ineffable slimness which seems the prerogative of ballet dancers: her skin had the flawless pallor and the texture of a magnolia blossom: her eyes really were the colour of sloes. In the summer of 1940, the Sadler's Wells Company went on tour through Holland. Germany and Holland were then at peace. No cloud had appeared in the particular bit of sky embracing those two countries. Then suddenly, not one, but many, clouds appeared above the city of Rotterdam. They were aeroplanes, and they killed thirty thousand people in two hours. The friendly Germans were offering their "protection" to this little people, who were their closest neighbours. Thus they demonstrated their "New Order". It was no world for the fragile figures of ballet dancers, and the Sadler's Wells Company had to fly. The story of their escape sounds like the scenario of a ballet.

The *Corps de Ballet* seems to have fluttered about for some hours at The Hague, not knowing which way to go. At last, the "Authorities" (those unseen powers whose voices fall, in times of crisis, like loud speakers from above) ordered them to get into a coach, which would convey them to a port. Darkness fell while they were travelling. Aeroplanes roared overhead, and the coach was ordered off the road. The Company found itself deposited before a dark, closed door, and they were told to "go into the hotel". They peered in. It was crowded. Not a crack remained, capable of holding the slimmest figure of a dancing girl. Besides which, the lounge smelt unpleasantly stuffy. The dancers decided that a night in the garden was more inviting; but as the night went on, it grew very chilly, and the girls huddled together, and shivered under their coats.

The place had the sweetly sounding name of *Velsen*, but in the thick darkness, nothing could be seen of it. Here and there, the shades of night were deepened by what seemed to be groups of great chestnut trees; and then again, the water of a tiny canal made a fleeting gleam of light. The girls walked about to keep warm, and their little footsteps disturbed birds or small animals, which scampered or flew away at the approach of these unaccustomed night-walkers.

Very gradually the dawn began, and an incredible sight was slowly revealed. The garden in which the ballet girls had passed the night must have belonged to a bird fancier. While the ashen twilight of morning still gave a ghostly quality to everything which it touched, movements all about, in the shrubs and trees, showed that life was awakening with the day. By degrees, these movements became visual, and then it could be seen that the garden was peopled with white birds. Ducks swooped on to the surface of the stream, and swam away leaving a shimmering line of white water in their wake. White pigeons peered from the pigeon cote, to soar upwards and to swirl round and round while their sleepy mates gurgled and coo'ed within. Big white pheasants crowed harshly as they suddenly woke, and then, with a loud rustle they left their roosting-places in the trees. Pure white cocks and hens walked quickly across the grass, as if bent on some important business, and a crowd of white turkeys began to gobble. A magnificent white peacock spread his tail, which followed behind him like an Emir's fan, as he made his royal progress through the grounds. A few seagulls flew rhythmically towards the coast; and down the little stream, one solitary black swan moved with supreme dignity and in complete silence, ignoring the presence of any other living creature in the garden.

Strangest of all, a little herd of white deer awoke, and, standing on their hind legs, they made their breakfast off the upper boughs of the shrubs.

I was spellbound by this amazing picture; and I could hardly listen to the story of the rest of that journey to England, though the other listeners found it very entertaining. I gathered that the *Corps de Ballet* had crossed on the upper deck of a Channel boat, from which vantage-ground they looked down upon the lower deck, packed with refugees, all very hungry. Like the ballet girls, they too had had nothing to eat for many hours, and now they showed great impatience at the length both of their journey and of their fast. I expect they felt even more impatient when, by one of those strange illusions well known to *Balletomanes*, the ballet Company floated over their heads on a bridge laid from the upper deck to the platform; and so they were the first to taste the homely and comforting cup of English strong tea, which seems to be offered to every returning exile.

Another girl at our party had been one of four English drivers attached to a Polish ambulance, operating in France during the spring of 1940. They spent most of April and May in what she described as "a hideous camp in lovely Brittany", where they felt that their war was, if anything, rather too peaceful. Most of the day, they waited for orders outside the hospital; and towards evening they were sent to collect sick or wounded from first aid posts scattered over a large area of beautiful country. They found the Polish officers quartered in pleasant roomy old châteaux, where they were invited to dine in the Messes before picking up their cases. They spent their off days wandering in the deep woods nearby, and sitting about with their books. They were quite cut off from the world, and knew absolutely nothing of the tragedy which was preparing in France. Life seemed to be a peaceful voyage down a quiet little stream; and when some Americans told them that the French were retreating, "their words seemed to them as idle tales". Then, one day, they saw a big Canadian convoy on its way inland from the coast; and a few days later, they met it again, coming back. The girl who was telling us the story knew one of these Canadian officers. It was the first of many unexpected meetings between old friends which occurred during those days when all the world seemed to be wandering about, lost. She went to him, and asked him where he was going. He was amazed to find her in this remote corner of France.

"What on earth are you doing here?" he asked.

She said she was driving an ambulance for the Polish Army.

"Get into my car and come with us. The French have gone, and I must get my men away. We had only just arrived. But you must leave at once. We'll hold up the transport for a bit, so that your party can join us."

This revelation was the first warning of danger which had reached the party, but it was quite impossible for the drivers to leave their unit. They decided, however, to return to their headquarters, and to ask to see the General. He sent his staff out of the room and said:

"Tell me what you know."

The driver then told him what she had heard from her Canadian friend, and the General replied that the Polish Army knew nothing at all of any French retreat. He told her to keep silent about this report, and then he took her to a small room where they found some of the staff. They drank glasses of Russian tea together, and all agreed that the Canadians must have been deceived by a fifth column rumour, and that what really was happening was that "*le Front approche*".

The party now returned to the headquarters of their ambulance, and found that other drivers, who had been sent out earlier in the day, had not returned. Everything seemed mysterious and unpleasant.

In the evening, in the little cafe where they usually had supper, they had another unexpected meeting with an old acquaintance. This was an English woman who had been sent over to bring back some A.T.S., who were manning a mobile canteen. She said, "You must come to St. Malo with us. The War Office has ordered all English women to leave France."

Now the Matron in charge of the ambulance was consulted, and she decided that they were under Polish orders, and could not go back to England without leave.

So the last link with home was broken, and the A.T.S. parry went away, saying as they left:

"Any message for your mother?"

"Only love."

That was the end of that. The four ambulance drivers felt that they were now the only English women left in France.

The sirens screeched all through the night, and in the morning, the Matron approached the Polish General, asking for further orders. The château occupied by the staff seemed completely normal. A butler and two footmen conducted them to a small drawing-room hung with priceless tapestry, in which the General, wearing a mackintosh, was bending over a map. He seemed preoccupied, and, without looking up, he said only five words:

"These ladies must not go."

That was the last they saw of him.

The ambulance party now seemed quite marooned. For one whole day, they sat calmly in the hospital, rolling bandages, and then the drivers received a fresh order. The hospital at Rennes was reported as being evacuated, and they were to drive there and secure any medical stores which might be left behind. Someone seemed to have decided that this unit should continue to face the enemy, in their corner of Brittany.

Rennes was an amazing sight. The enormous camp outside the town was deserted, leaving only one sentry at the gate. Food remained uneaten on the tables, and half-cooked in the kitchens. Clothes were littered on the ground, and letters lay on the tables. Columns of black smoke hung over the town, and when they reached the barracks to which they were sent to find the medical stores, no one seemed to have time to attend to them. The town itself had become a dead town. Footsteps echoed in the silent streets, which looked as long-ago deserted as the empty streets of Pompeii. The story of that day, and of the following ones, was like a confused nightmare.

There was the sudden apparition, in the empty streets of Rennes, of four British soldiers with blackened faces and clothes, asking, in a broad Lancashire dialect, for the ambulance to carry away some wounded from a train which had just been blown up in the station. There was the hospital ward crowded with wounded, many of them only half bandaged, with no one to attend to them. And at last there was the room where the medical stores—tons of them—were found at last, and in which, as they came in, a telephone bell was pealing. They lifted the receiver.

"Evacuate at once."

Now, everything the ambulances could hold was hastily hurled into them. Aeroplanes roared above them as they drove back thus laden; and then they were told to return at once to save more stores from falling into enemy hands. Before they could start, the Germans were already in the town.

A night of confusion followed. Five or six times, they had orders to pack their ambulances and to be ready to leave at once. Five or six times came the order to unpack and go to bed. The Major ordered them to leave. The Colonel forbade it. The Major left. The Colonel said that no nurses must follow his example. The Matron waited ready to obey orders from the Polish staff, but none were issued. Meanwhile the men were seeping away, and by morning the camp was almost empty. Then the milkman appeared, bringing with him his normal peace-time atmosphere. He left a pint of milk, and went off whistling. The nurses filled their thermos flasks for any emergency. They seemed to be almost alone, but at any rate, they had stayed together. A few officers were still in the camp to decide on what action should be taken, and when, but they had absolutely no outside intelligence to guide them.

At about eleven o'clock in the morning, a tiny car arrived, driven by a French officer, who, when he saw them, said most emphatically:

"*You must go.* Being British you will be taken prisoners at once, the Germans are now two miles off."

Again the Matron went to seek orders from the Polish authorities and when she came back, she said, with her eyes fixed on the ground, "We can leave at once". Even then she had probably received no, definite orders. These Poles had been left, like Casabianca, with orders to stay where they were, and they could not bring themselves to give in. But now the English drivers leapt into the ambulances and shot out of the gates on to the road to Bordeaux.

The crowded French roads during those weeks of the Retreat, have been often described; and on these, there were also the three thousand Poles from their own camp, as well as many men of the French Air Force, trying to get to England. These men kept hanging on to the back of the ambulances so as to get a short lift on their way. Now the ambulances were warned not to go on to Nantes, which was already in enemy hands, but to turn west for St. Nazaire. The Loire there is very wide, and it was expected that the French might make a stand on this river, for there seemed to be a touching faith in an old prophecy that this was where the enemy would be checked.

At St. Nazaire, while they were asking for the transport officer to give them a pass over the Loire ferry, an English tommy said, "Excuse me, Madam, I think I have seen you before". It was yet another unexpected rencontre. This was an ex-footman of Lady Cunard's, and as they waited for this life and death permission to cross into safety, they conversed politely about the many friends they used to meet in Grosvenor Square in the old days.

Suddenly it was announced that the last ferry-boat would leave in five minutes' time, from the far end of the town. The drivers sprang to their seats, and dashed at full speed through the streets, arriving with three minutes to spare. The runway was already packed with cars, but the ambulances had priority which they hoped would carry them through. Eight or nine other cars were in the same (as they hoped) fortunate position, but now they all got into a hopeless block. The cars were so crowded together, that if anyone moved an inch, there was an alarming sound of breaking mudguards, in spite of which, people continued to move on, leaving torn-off fragments of their cars behind. Many screaming hysterical Frenchwomen added to the pandemonium, and in this impossible position they stayed, not for the expected three minutes, but for eighteen maddening hours.

When they were almost in despair, there appeared on the scene a padre who had been blown up in the train at Rennes, and had since walked to St. Nazaire. At the same moment some British soldiers arrived. Their ship had been sunk in the port, and they now had no clothes at all. Some were promptly found among the stores in the ambulance, and in these the padre clothed the men, and he then took them off with him to cross by boat, taking also the young Polish nurses, who were a great responsibility to the ambulance party. The English drivers remained on the runway, being told by the French that if the Germans approached, they must at once put on mufti and walk down the road to meet them, saying that they were Americans who had been left behind.

It was now getting dark, and they unpacked an enormous ham from their stores, which they shared with everyone within reach. This was quite a gay episode. All night, a distracting and extraordinary noise went on—the screaming sound of a machine cutting steel in the dock nearby, where a ship was still actually being built. And all night too, explosions shook the town.

When darkness was at its deepest, a French officer gave them orders to empty the ambulance, and to move it where it could be set up as a barricade. No sooner was this done than a terrific raid began, and they all had to crawl under the ambulance, where strange faces met strange faces in a still stranger proximity. The Matron was now very calm and encouraging. She had been under fire before.

During the night, they were told to put their civilian clothes under their uniform, in case they had to appear suddenly in mufti; and then they were informed they would leave by the first morning ferry-boat. They distributed some of their tinned food among the French soldiers, who opened the tins with their bayonets, and swallowed the contents without cooking; and then the exhausted drivers snatched some uneasy sleep in their ambulances.

Early in the morning the ferry began to work, but every time the boat appeared, the ambulances were crowded out. They shared the fete of the Sick Man at the Pool at Bethesda, whose experience was that "While I am coming, another steppeth down before me". They were pushed out every time, by cars which wrenched away parts of any vehicles in their path, in order to break through and reach the ferry-boat first. It was chaos.

Now there reappeared their friend the padre, and he soon got into touch with a transport officer, who combed out the cars ahead and placed them second in the rank, saying that the next boat would be the last to cross. It was an unbelievable moment. The eighteen hours of that frantic struggle were ended. They moved freely on to the ferry, and were carried calmly across the river. What did it matter to them that they were received on the other side by a fresh raid, with bombs falling all round them? It felt no more alarming than a short sharp rainstorm.

The padre now mounted the front seat of the ambulance, and guided them to La Rochelle. On either side of the road, the ditches were piled up with cars which had run out of petrol, and so had been abandoned. The heat now grew so intense that the Matron could no longer bear the journey in that oven-like ambulance, with every garment she possessed packed upon her back. She made them stop while she took off some of her superfluous layers of clothes, and while this was going on, came another unexpected meeting. A woman's voice hailed them: "What can I do for you?"

It was the head of the committee, under which they had worked when they first reached Paris, a time which now seemed a century before.

This lady escorted them to the *Mairie*, and to look for the various town officials who could help them to get away. Every office was empty. All had gone to the port. They followed to the quay-side, where they were taken to the transport officer, who greeted them with these crushing words:

"You are too late. The British Navy has gone. You must go on to Bordeaux."

It was vain to reply that they had no petrol left, and that an attempted journey to Bordeaux must inevitably land them in one of those roadside ditches, among those abandoned cars. This did seem the end.

But at this darkest moment, it appeared that the British Navy had not gone. It was still there. It always will be.

Two British naval officers arrived. They were still combing the country for any English left behind; and they said that their ships were leaving immediately from a point five miles away. "Can you quickly collect all your party?"

But when they heard that the party consisted partly of six Polish nurses, then the officers looked rather blank. Their orders were to collect only British subjects. No foreigners at all. However, nothing really disturbed their control of the situation. They told the drivers to come with them, and to explain the case to the Captain; and if he consented, the nurses could then be brought on board.

Now they had to smash up their ambulances and to get into the officers' boat, leaving the nurses behind. It was agony to do this, and everyone on shore seemed to be weeping, but the calmness of those naval officers was a tower of strength.

When they reached the ship, they were at once fortified by some cups of that famous strong black tea, which they drank while the Captain sent back for the nurses, and also for some Jewish girls who were with them. They had literally been the last party to be brought away; and now they were packed cosily like sardines on the floor of a cabin, and they were told that they would leave at midnight. There was a great sense of safety in being subject to the time-table of a British warship: no more would three minutes turn into eighteen hours. They were ordered to sail at midnight. And they did.

The experienced Matron now pronounced that the ship might possibly be sunk on the voyage, and she instructed her flock to take off their skirts and prepare to swim. During those stormy three days in the Bay of Biscay, modesty and security came uppermost by turns. Those skirts were taken off and on, according to whichever was predominant at any given moment. The passengers expected to be taken to Liverpool, but on the voyage, the Captain decided on Plymouth, and they landed at that port at six o'clock one morning. No one was there to meet them, for they had been despaired of by their families.

As I listened to the story of the Polish ambulance drivers, I was watching a young airman, who seemed disinclined to talk of his own experiences. His round boyish face was made for gaiety and fun, and he listened with appreciation to what the others said. But all the time, there was a shadow in his eyes. He did not want to remember what he himself had gone through in those very same weeks. I knew about him, for his mother was for many months one of my lodgers. He had belonged to that heroic squadron which spent six weeks on a frozen lake within the Arctic Circle in the north part of Norway, during that desperate spring of 1940.

Twice over had these boys flown eighteen Gladiators across the North Sea to hold the Luftwaffe with their gallant onslaughts. The first expedition lasted only five days. At the end of that time, the eighteen planes were reduced to five, although not one of them was brought down in combat. The squadron had been obliged to go to Norway in a fleet of out-of-date, and practically obsolete, machines, which were all that could be spared at the time to face the most modern and powerful German aircraft of the day. The Gladiator squadron found that the frozen lake was completely exposed to the enemy with no possible shelter, or means of keeping the planes out of sight. The Norwegians could offer no other site. At night the cold was so intense, that it sometimes took hours to start the engines, and the poor old machines were often stuck helplessly on the ground, exposed to attack from the air. The Germans must greatly have enjoyed bombing these out-of-action non-combatants; for whenever the British squadron did manage to send up one or two machines to face the overwhelming numbers of the enemy, by sheer brilliancy of flying, they fought the Germans out of the sky, without losing in battle a single plane. The thirteen aircraft which failed to return to England after this first expedition were all put out of action, either by engine breakdowns, or by being bombed when they were unable to fly. Their officers burnt the remains of the machines they left behind, so that no parts could be of use to the enemy. Then they patched up their last five machines with spare parts mostly taken from German planes which they had brought down. So they made their way home leaving the Luftwaffe twenty-nine planes the worse off for their visit.

In less than three weeks these pilots returned with another eighteen Gladiators, to demonstrate once more that the German superiority in machines was more than outmatched by the British superiority in skill. For another fortnight, they continued the unequal conflict: unequal, because the Germans had now got such a wholesome fear of these Gladiator pilots, that they could very seldom be compelled to stay up for a fight.

Now the Englishmen were called home to share in the Battle of Britain. This time there were ten Gladiators left, though most of them were patchwork machines made out of parts collected again from shot-down planes. These gallant wrecks, with their still more gallant pilots, were put on board the *Glorious*, and two hours after they left Norway, the aircraft-carrier was sunk by enemy action. All those boys were drowned.

Two pilots out of the original eighteen had been left behind to bring over the ground staffs, and the crews of the planes which did not return. One of these two was the boy in my house. As he heard the others talking, he seemed haunted by the memory of those few, that happy few, that band of brothers now beneath the North Sea. He did not tell his own story, but when somebody asked him about Norway, he said he couldn't think how anyone could wish to go there on a holiday to see the midnight sun.

"It is much too light," he said, "with its everlasting shining. And you never can tell whether it is three o'clock in the morning or three o'clock in the afternoon."

He said no more about it.

When I overheard what one of the guests at this party said about Dunkirk, I felt, more than ever, that the whole thing was miraculous, an "Act of God," in the words of the old verdict at inquests, in the face of an inexplicable event. Someone in France planned the evacuation of the British Army, though he could never have known whether or not his plan would come off. He had somehow to arrange that those scattered thousands of men should be moved to the coast; though once there, he could not tell what might become of them. Then each brigade, each battalion, each unit, and sometimes each individual must make his way as best he could, knowing nothing of the plan and perhaps simply remembering the words: "Theirs not to reason why."

Meanwhile, across the Channel, someone else was planning the counter-move. He suddenly called upon hundreds of little craft—excursion steamers, yachts, fishing-boats, river motor-boats, even rowing-boats, to leave, within an hour, their peace-time moorings in seas, rivers, streams, or canals, and to embark upon some important national work. They were not told what it was. On both sides, these moves were made in total darkness; by which I do not only mean the darkness of ignorance, but the darkness of night. This blindfold pilgrimage calls to mind the Blind Man in the Gospel—*I see men as trees walking.*

But when my lodger spoke of his own party and their stumbling trek, I learnt that he was not one of those who "left everything behind". He possessed something which he could not leave.

Orders came from the Brigade Major that his small unit of about forty men must proceed at once to Dunkirk. It was the late twilight of a June evening, and everyone had immediately to shoulder his kit and be off. My officer was ready to leave everything behind except *himself*, and that self did not only consist of so many feet of flesh, blood, and bones, equipped with boots and uniform, razor and revolver, tooth-brush and cigarettes. It included the outward and visible sign of his making into an officer, in a special technical corps. With him were the books containing the notes on his studies during the past three years. It was the new personality which had been built around him, by his training from the time he left school. He was not going to leave that behind. He valued it too highly, and no doubt the Germans would value it still more. He put the books into his pack and swung it on his back. Yes. It was heavy, but not too heavy to carry for the two and a half miles which they were told was the distance to Dunkirk.

The night was far darker than seemed justified by actual clock time. It was a darkness which could be felt, hanging over them like a heavy black substance, and it soon explained itself. The sky was completely hidden by columns of rolling black smoke. Behind them very far away, was a red glow which now and again flamed up suddenly. If those fires were in Dunkirk, it was much more than two and a half miles away. Towards these fires, the little party groped their way through the blinding black pall. Quite nearby, a battery suddenly began firing. Bang. Bang. Bang. Was it our own, or the enemy's? They hesitated. Finally the guns stopped. The party went on. Now they were on a deserted beach, beyond which there seemed to be boats out at sea. A voice from nowhere called instructions. Were they reliable! They ignored them.

The two and a half miles turned into seventeen, and with every mile, the pack of books grew heavier. That load was hell; and at each halt the same half-submerged question pushed itself to the surface. "What can I do with these confounded books; Bury them? Hide them? Burn them? How? or where?" There was no answer, except to shoulder the books once more, although, like the Old Man of the Sea, they almost broke the back that bore them.

Now the darkness took a new shape. It became a queue of soldiers, a full mile long, and mumbling to one another in the French language. The bombs and fires were now quite near—too near to be pleasant, for this really was Dunkirk. The seventeen miles trek was over, and they were on the pier, among dead and dying men. The night had been so fantastic that it seemed that it could hardly be real life. Yet, it was.

They marshalled their men on to a waiting destroyer, and as they stumbled on board, they found an unbelievable welcome in the shape of a pint of beer for every man. It was pure nectar; but they could hardly swallow it, still less appreciate it as it deserved, before they were overpowered by sleep. Dover came too soon, for there they must pull themselves together and step off the boat. It was surprising to find people expecting them, waiting for them, and evidently thinking they were not complete failures. The strong cup of tea was now provided, with other refreshments, by a party of women; and one strange kind old man received our officer with a telegram form in his hand which he wrote out and addressed to his parents telling them that he was safe and at home.

There was no doubt that the general favourite at our party to-day was a young man who had been a wireless operator in a merchant ship, lately sunk by enemy action. She was carrying over five thousand passengers including troops and hospital staff when she was torpedoed, and, although the ship went to the bottom, less than two hundred of those on board were drowned. Our wireless operator had been on duty in the middle watch of the night, when a colossal report resounded, and a huge explosion shook the ship. All the officers at once reported to the Captain, to receive their orders; and among them came the Chief Engineer. In everyday tones, he now *regretted to report* that the engine-room had been hit, and the damage was serious. The ship was obviously in imminent danger. As the Engineer finished his report, the Captain's eye fell on him.

"Good God, Chief," he said. "What is the matter with the top of your head?"

Everyone turned to look.

The Chief Engineer's cap was wobbling up and down in the most extraordinary manner.

"It's only ma twa canaries. I thocht they'd be safer in ma cap then in their cage."

Here, then, was another man who would not leave everything behind, whatever the enemy might be doing.

Everyone now hastened to boat stations and, on the way, the wireless operator met the storekeeper hurrying along with, in his hand, a moving sack, tied with a piece of string.

"What the hell have you got in there?" he asked genially, as I am sure he would.

"These are my three tabbies. I am not going to leave them behind for anyone," said the storekeeper, while a harsh catawaul from inside proved that the three tabbies were by no means quiescent in their sack.

Everyone now took to the boats; and as the last boat moved away from the ship several more cats were seen crowding together on the deck with fire blazing behind them. No Englishman could resist these panic-stricken animals. The boat swung round again and went near enough to the ship for all the cats to spring to safety.

The wireless operator was stationed in a boat which was supposed to accommodate sixty-five people, but which was soon crowded with ninety. Unfortunately it immediately appeared that the little engine was out of order, so the various men on board took turns with two pairs of sculls, which was all they had in the way of navigation. They worked very hard for eleven hours, and thus they kept the boat's head in the right direction, and saved her from shipping water, and so from sinking.

Shortly after they left the liner, there passed them, in the sea, a valiant little nurse, swimming for all she was worth towards a raft just beyond them. As she approached it, a voice from it called out to her:

"We are full. Better swim to the next raft."

Not in the least disturbed, a small treble voice trilled out:

"O.K. How far?" and on she swam into the night.

It was a relief to learn that the next raft was more hospitable and welcomed her cordially.

When the order was given to "Abandon Ship", it was expected that she was on the point of sinking, but it was not till nearly morning when the boat-crews watched her last moments.

Like other vessels in war-time, she had been painted a battleship grey, and now, while all eyes looked on from the boats, a miracle took place. The grey garment fell away, pealed off by the intense heat, and for one brief moment before she went down, the original colours came back in all their purity, and the ghost of the long-lost peace-time ship shone out in her gay holiday dress. Just for a few seconds, and then she heeled over on her side, and vanished from sight. From all the boats, they watched her go. It was a poignant moment, especially for the Captain, who had sailed in her from the day she was launched. It was like the vision of the bride in her wedding dress, appearing to the eyes of a husband watching at his wife's death-bed. So will Beauty find a way to clothe Tragedy, till the heart is uplifted and comforted. The lovely ship left her last message behind: "I do not leave you with the picture of dismal war before your eyes, but of something more truly my own—my gay and gallant colours of Peace."

Chapter X

NO BELLS TO-NIGHT

Ring out, wild bells, to the wild sky,
  The flying clouds, the frosty light,
  The year is dying in the night;
Ring out, wild bells, and let him die.

Ring out the old, ring in the new,
  Ring, happy bells, across the snow:
  The year is going, let him go:
Ring out the false, ring in the true.

Ring out the want, the care, the sin,
  The faithless coldness of the times;
  Ring out, ring out, my mournful rhymes,
But let the fuller minstrel in.

Ring out old shapes of foul disease;
  Ring out the narrowing lust of gold;
  Ring out the thousand wars of old,
Ring in the thousand years of peace.

Ring in the valiant man and free,
  The larger heart, the kindlier hand;
  Ring out the darkness of the land,
Ring in the Christ that is to be.

There, in those verses, is New Year's Eve, as it was when we were children. The first four lines of Tennyson's poem exactly recall the keen, clear, brilliant voices of the bells, as they swung free among the flying clouds. There was nothing human in that music, although it was made by men. It was a festival of the universe. I believe that, even then, people in other places were making merry at balls and parties, but we were merrier than they, and also nearer to life. We stood in the village street, with, over our heads, this music miraculously and for ever out of reach. The music-makers were invisible—bell-ringers and carollers both hidden in the church tower. It was exciting and supernatural.

But it was not many years before a new sound crashed in to interrupt the harmony. Then, when we opened the door to let the New Year in, we found that the bells and the carol-singers had monstrous rivals—the sirens in the factories of the nearest town. Who can have been the first to conceive of anything so frightful as this mocking travesty of the angelic music of the spheres? It seemed to be a hideous uprush of discord from the underworld. And yet, for years, civilised people tolerated it as an appropriate greeting for the opening year.

To-night, as I watched the New Year in, I heard no sound at all. Only the stars looked in at my window. The bells have been silent for over three years (except for two blessed occasions), and the sirens, for the same length of time, have been put into what is surely their more appropriate place—only allowed to speak as presages of an expected and diabolical visitor. To-night we were alone with the stars, and I think that when the war is over, and we joyfully hear the bells again, we shall beg for the sirens to return to their rightful work as only factory time-keepers.

This train of thought came into my mind when I was walking in the Park to-night. My lodgers were at their various parties, and I had spent the evening at a Parish Whist Drive, which ended early, as old-fashioned country parties always do. Whether the day be the first or the last of the year, village people must get up early in the morning; and they know that a late night makes a bad start next day. How wise they are! and how near to Nature, the Nature of the birds and beasts and flowers, who follow, as closely as possible, the setting sun, in the choice of their bed-time! So our whist drive ended well before ten. We gave the prizes—parcels of groceries, packets of cigarettes, a pottery vase or two. Then came a few New Year wishes, spoken with a deeper intent than in ordinary years; and after this, the assembly drifted out into the lane, casually talking over the events of the evening, or perhaps the events of the past year. I drifted with them, but I soon left them behind, as I had farther to go than most.

Then followed my own secret and very beautiful farewell to the year 1942, and not only to that particular calendar year, but to a year in my own personal life. For this day had been my birthday.

At the Park gate, I was challenged by a sentry—that most romantic of ceremonies.

"Who goes there?"

"Friend."

"Advance, friend, and be recognised."

Now came two or three steps forward, into the tiny circle of light from the sentry's torch, so that my face and my identity card could be scrutinised. My appearance was, of course, quite familiar to the guards, but the regulations must be obeyed. I passed the test, and then, with "A happy New Year" on either side, I went on alone into the darkness of the Park. "Time and the hour" were left outside.

Here was the old familiar darkness which I had known from childhood, and only in one thing did it differ from the New Year's Eves of the old days. That silence. "There are no bells to-night." Those words occur in a little poem written by one of my lodgers when he was on duty on a Christmas Eve during the war. He was then struck, as I was to-night, by the fact that the silent bells still do speak to those who knew and loved them of old. Yes. No one is ringing the bells to-night, but how beautifully they still fill the silence.

Above me shone Orion, my best-loved constellation, covering the whole heaven with his proud stride, and, glittering beside him, hung his sword. Many other stars shone all round, but none so bright as he. These celestial sentinels, watching over distances far beyond our ken, awake in one an eternal confidence. I remembered the Bethlehem shepherds, who kept watch over their flocks by night, and yet had spirits free for star-gazing. They guarded their sheep none the worse for that.

The star canopy was still spread above me when I reached home; and when I put out my light and opened my bedroom window, there was Orion, still watching. Thoughts from him seemed to stream down upon me.

My mind passed from those shepherds of nearly two thousand years ago, to a man living on this island in this very autumn, who also had an all-day job, and, like the shepherds, his all-day included all-night. He is an inshore fisherman; and because many of the deep-sea fishermen are now catching mines (a kind of fish which is more than "ticklish"), men like Mr. Ellis are busier than ever, and they produce a far larger proportion than before of the fish we eat in this country. But the eyes of this fisherman were not glued upon his lobster-pots and fishing-nets. He remains, what he was before, an amateur astronomer. So nightly, throughout the war, he has continued to search the sky. Then, on the 12th of November in this year of 1942. he, as usual, turned his telescope heavenwards. He saw a wonder. A new star shone brilliantly out. Till that night, it had never before been seen by man, though it may have existed, invisible to us, for millions of years. Such a moment has occurred in the life of very few men. To witness the birth of a star! How immeasurably wider one's universe would become after that apparition! Even

> "Stout Cortez, when with eagle eyes
> He stared at the Pacific,"

might envy this

> "Watcher of the skies
> When some new planet swept into his ken";

for the discovery *Nova Puppis* did not bring into our sphere a new ocean to be fought over.

Mr. Ellis carefully noted the exact position of his discovery and the hour when he made it, and he immediately telegraphed these to the Observatory at Greenwich. Within a few hours, the existence of the new star was also reported to Greenwich from Sweden, so the find was doubly proved.

There is to-day, in some quarters, a return to the old custom of consulting astrologers, in order to learn what they think of the immediate future course of the war. How jejune such probing seems to be in face of this flaming new Creation which will blaze in the sky for who knows how many aeons!

So it must have seemed to Mr. Ellis, who nevertheless couldn't help remembering that in June 1918 another new star, *Nova Aquila*, had also been discovered. Did that presage the end of the last war, which took place five months later? The last thing which such a man as Mr. Ellis would wish to do, would be to harness his own breath-taking discovery on to a date in history; yet the idea did occur to him. It occurred, and passed through his mind, leaving his own star to shine for ever in his consciousness. Come what might, in the future, for him, he knew that he had found his star.

On the night of my birthday, two months later, I lay in bed and watched Orion very slowly moving through space—a space vast enough for his passage to be unimpeded by however many new stars might be born in the heavens. Such are the major happenings in the universe of which we are a part. We too move in the world of Orion and of Nova Puppis. Mr. Ellis moves consciously in it. His kinship with the stars is a part of his daily life, and this must surely put all earthly happenings into their true perspective. Yet we, who only read about his great discovery, must surely be uplifted by it too. We go on living our workaday lives, and so does he; but I, for one, felt that to know that day, as one swept a room, that there was a new light in the sky, must surely do something to "make that and the action fine".

All fishermen are not astronomers, nor are all war-workers, miners, munition-makers, wardens, or members of the Home Guard. And we all sometimes find ourselves, our backs bent over some rather exhausting piece of work, with, sounding in our ears, the ancient and restless question: "*Watchman, will the night soon pass?*" We are misled if we think that the answer is written in the calendar or on the wrist-watch. We are wiser not to trouble over the actual date of that answer, but, instead, to watch Nature working beside us, regardless of our questioning. Mr. Ellis has his telescope to "take his mind off" his work, but all Nature-lovers can call on the same source for the strengthening which comes from change of scene and interest. We need not even go so far as to "ask of the stars in motion":

"Not where the wheeling systems darken,
And out benumbed conceiving soars!—
The drift of pinions, could we harken,
    Beats at our own clay-shuttered doors.

"The angels keep their ancient places;—
    Turn but a stone, and start a wing!
'Tis ye, 'tis your estrangéd faces,
    That miss the many-splendoured thing."

I have found that the happiest way to carry on in the war is, not to worry about any immediate effect of what we are actually doing, but to do it as well as we can, and then to look away and watch nature all around, slowly reaching her effortless and sure fruition. That is the complete change of air and scene which we so often think we must have. There is no repose like the realisation that one's little daily drudgery is already a part of something beyond itself. That was the climax of Dante's vision of the Paradiso:

But yet the will roll'd onward, like a wheel
In even motion, by the love impell'd,
That moves the sun in heaven and all the stars.

For indeed we can rejoice in the sight of Nature at work, even without looking so far as to the place where new stars are born.
    Think, for instance, of this year's harvest. Practically the whole

of the man- and woman-power in the country had already been taken into the War effort, either on the battle-field, on the ocean, in the air, or in the factory. The farms were terribly short of labour. Farmers took off their coats and worked harder than ever. Old men came back into their own, proud to know that the fields where they had worked "from a boy" were still in need of their feeble but experienced hands. Land girls and schoolboys brought youth and gaiety to the harvest fields. And Mother Earth responded as never before. In spite of our permanent gibes at the uncertainty of our weather, it was proved that the English soil and the English climate do understand each other, and get on very well together. It was little short of a miracle that the harvest of 1942, worked by emergency staffs, and temporary staffs, and amateur staffs, should have been a "record" one.

Said a neighbouring farmer to me this autumn:

"We have had the greatest harvest within the memory of man. And more. *It has been the greatest harvest, time out of memory.* It is the richest harvest that England has ever known. When we speak of 'the memory of man', we mean the memory of our fathers and grandfathers, of men whom we ourselves have spoken to, or whose experience has come down to us by word of mouth. That generally means about a hundred years, or a little more. Back to the early nineteenth century. Till then, English harvests had always been very far below our average to-day. Modern methods of culture have immensely increased the productiveness of our soil. A 'record' harvest before 'the memory of man' meant a very small fraction of what we had this year. That is what we English soil has done for us while we are all working short-handed."

To let one's mind dwell upon this does not hinder our everyday work. It merely reminds us of our countless invisible fellow workers. Plague and blight may be enemies who may sometimes invade our fields and gardens, but "they that be with us are more than they that be with them".

This year, the leaves stayed golden on the beeches till early in December. It seems a small thing to remember when such stirring events were also taking place. Mr. Churchill reminded us that

"November is usually a month of fog and gloom", but that this year it was "a month in which our soldiers and sailors and airmen have been victorious, in which our gallant Russian allies have struck redoubtable blows against the common enemy, in which our American allies and our kith and kin far-off in the Pacific have also seen their efforts crowned with a considerable measure of success. A great month, this last month of November."

Yes. It was a great month; but while the blood flows faster at the recital of these gallant deeds, it is still memorable that the crimson and copper of the beeches were around us till after the end of what had been in no sense, this year, "a month of fog and gloom".

I always read the paragraphs called "The Course of Nature", which appear in *The Times* once or twice a week. They prove the existence of many people who still watch Nature with curious and understanding eyes, and for whom "her ways are ways of pleasantness, and all her paths are peace". I think these are the wise people, nor need they necessarily be the idle and unpractical. They, like Mr. Ellis with his telescope, have possibly got "a full-time job" as well; and, like him, they see life in its true proportions. They may be Home Guards, or fire-watchers, or wardens, but their work does not prevent them from hearing a new bird sing, or from catching the scent of a flower which blows earlier than its time.

Because I had also observed it, I was particularly interested in the many writers who, in all parts of England, had heard the spring song of the thrushes quite early in the past autumn. They wrote from Lancashire and Cornwall, from Wiltshire, Surrey, and Sussex, from Hampshire, Buckinghamshire, and Oxford. All these songs were both intermittent and recurrent. After a night of deluge in October, my own garden had been startled by a sudden joyous gush of thanksgiving. It was the song my thrushes always begin in the week round Christmas Day. Then came a silence of a week or so, before the same songs began again. These out-of-season songs were so unusual and striking that they were noted down by bird-lovers in all those scattered districts. And some of these same observers had detected the scent of the winter heliotrope many weeks before it was to be expected; while, in Scotland, the late summer flowers, like dahlias and nasturtium, bloomed on till they were met by the early spring arrivals.

That is the happiness of living in this place, and indeed in any country place in England to-day. We are not cut off from the life-and-death struggle of our country, for has not this been called "a war of little groups", in which the Home Guards and the housewives take their place behind the aircraft and the tanks? Yet we still live on in our own homes, and if other homes are like mine (as I am sure they are) it is still possible for a visitor to say, as he enters our doors, "Here, one can hardly realise the war". And that is perhaps the best thing we can ever give to the strangers within our gates.

So the colour of the trees still matters to us, and also to our lodgers. It has mattered to us—spring, summer, autumn, and winter—all through the past three years; and, as for the winters, it must be admitted that the war ones have been very hard. They really might have been planned by Hitler. Yet, in spite of that, now they have taken their place among the visual memories of a lifetime, what rare effects of beauty some of them are found to recall! There was that marvellous Sunday morning when the rain froze as it fell, and the trees were suddenly hung with tinkling icicles, chiming with little ghost-like echoes of the church bells which had long been silent. There are no icicles to-night, and there are no bells; but "there's night and day, brother, both sweet things; sun, moon and stars, brother, all sweet things; there's likewise the wind on the heath. Life is very sweet, brother."

Lightning Source UK Ltd.
Milton Keynes UK
UKOW02f0332290116

267373UK00003B/49/P